A WISCONSIN TRAILS GUIDE

UP NORTH
WISCONSIN
A REGION FOR ALL SEASONS

SHARYN ALDEN

WISCONSIN TRAILS
Madison, Wisconsin

Library of Congress Catalog Card Number: 99-70830
ISBN: 0-915024-69-1

Editor: Stan Stoga
Designer: Kathie Campbell
Printed in the United States of America
First edition, first printing

Photo credits: Cover, Jeff Richter, Iron County, Wisconsin;
pp. 82 (lower) and 83, Barb and Min Grossi; pp. 135 and 145 (lower), Craig Locey;
p. 149, Sim Ashlock; all others, Sharyn Alden

Wisconsin Tales and Trails, Inc.
P.O. Box 5650
Madison, WI 53705
(800) 236-8088
info@wistrails

UP NORTH WISCONSIN

Scale

0   20   40 Miles

0   20   40 Kilometers

Apostle Islands National Lakeshore

Lake Superior

MICHIGAN

MINNESOTA

Lac du Flambeau Ind. Res.

Northern Highland-American Legion State Forest

Chequamegon National Forest

Bad River Ind. Res.

Chequamegon National Forest

Lac Courte Oreilles Ind. Res.

Nicolet National Forest

Menominee Ind. Res.

Stockbridge Ind. Res.

Timms Hill Highest Point

Rib Mtn.

Menominee R.

Peshtigo R.

Wolf R.

Wisconsin R.

Trempealeau R.

Chippewa R.

St. Croix R.

Apple R.

Green Bay

Counties and places

Superior, Douglas, Bayfield, Iron River, Cable, Hayward, Washburn, Burnett, Shell Lake, Grantsburg, St. Croix Falls, Polk, Rice Lake, Barron, Barron, Shell Lake, Menomonie, Dunn, St. Croix, Hudson, River Falls, Prescott, Pierce

Bayfield, Ashland, Mellen, Hurley, Iron, Mercer, Phillips, Price, Ladysmith, Rusk, Sawyer, Taylor, Medford, Chippewa, Chippewa Falls, Eau Claire

Florence, Florence, Forest, Crandon, Langlade, Antigo, Lincoln, Merrill, Marathon, Wausau, Oneida, Rhinelander, Minocqua, Eagle River, Vilas, Tomahawk

Marinette, Marinette, Crivitz, Oconto, Brown, Green Bay, Shawano, Keshena, Stockbridge

N · E · W · S

contents

introduction

I n May 1997, when Wisconsin Public Television's *WeekEnd* show asked its viewers the question "Where does northern Wisconsin begin?" the program was deluged with phone calls. Among the tremendous number of responses, there were some half-hearted answers, such as "Portage" (presumably because of the big sign in the city park proclaiming that this is "Where the North Begins") and "anywhere above Beloit." Most callers, however, agreed that the southern boundary of northern Wisconsin—or the North Woods or "Up North"—is marked by Highway 64, which runs from Marinette on the east, zigzags through Antigo, Merrill, and near Bloomer, and ends at the St. Croix River.

I was also intrigued by the question and eager to see whether the callers were on target. And so I embarked on a year-and-a-half quest to report on the region's noteworthy forests, lakes, rivers, inns, restaurants, entertainment spots, museums, and historical points of interest, all the while staying connected with the spirit of the North Woods.

When I first tackled the question, I followed the lead of the show's callers and set Highway 64 as the southern boundary. Later, after I had driven more than 20,000 miles throughout the area, I had to shift the border to Highway 29, which parallels 64 across the state about 15 to 20 miles to the south. The reason for the change of heart was that the area between the two roads contained too many "North Woodsy" sights and stops to be ignored. Of course, none of this is really important because Up North is also a state of mind. Yet boundaries help as reference points.

After countless trips throughout northern Wisconsin, I began to feel as if I were coming home when I smelled the fresh pines, cool night air, and crisp smoke from campfires and old lodge fireplaces. When four-lane roads became two lanes, when stoplights were fewer, when another lake appeared at every bend, and when crickets harmonized in symphonic choruses, I knew I was in the middle of the North Woods. When I crossed the mighty Wisconsin River several times, all the while transfixed by its beautiful blue lagoons, pools, and sandbars, my spirits soared. I was coming closer to where I had "left off" the last time I wandered through the region. Some clues to the northern Wisconsin ambiance were dead giveaways. In Antigo, there was the sign that read "Squirrel Tails Wanted," and another near Minocqua announcing "Leeches $9.50 a Pound," and still another near Hayward alerting drivers on Highway 77 to watch for elk. These were indeed confirmations that I was Up North.

Is This Heaven?

For over 20 years I have been trekking across the globe covering popular as well as remote destinations for newspapers and magazines. As one who was born and raised in Wisconsin, I have long felt privileged to return to the glorious diversity of my home state. If you've got to leave the beaches of Bali, the pristine beauty of the Swiss Alps, Africa's sweeping plains, or the wonders of Ephesus, then Wisconsin is, believe it or not, heaven—a marvelous place to come home to.

So it was that I took on the assignment of logging miles in my home state in order to give you useful information about Wisconsin's North Woods. Having spent many summers (and holidays) growing up in the area, I felt I knew it fairly well. However, I found out that I had much to learn about the state's northern territory and, consequently, I discovered many towns and scenic areas previously unfamiliar to me. I had never seen Wisconsin's Concrete Park in Phillips, for instance; and I was so taken by Fred Smith's amazing ability to build folk art statues from cement, old glass, and beer bottles, an art he had begun when he was 65, I went back to the park several times. My fascination is reflected in the fact that in the book I devote a few more words than usual to Fred and his unique craftsmanship. Similarly, a few other captivating sights and scenes I encountered get a bit more attention than others. I hope readers will share my enthusiasm for these spots and forgive my occasional lapse in journalistic objectivity.

It was a labor of love, exploring and recording my findings, over many trips back and forth Up North. On almost all of my treks, I was alone, but there were a few exceptions.

My son, Sim, joined me on two Wolf River rafting expeditions near Langlade and again sailing in the Apostle Islands. My friends Burt and Karen Scheele joined me for pie at the Norske Nook in Osseo, then bravely took part in some of my wanderings around Hudson and St. Croix Falls. After faithfully following my directions over many winding roads that twisted and turned in ways that looked different than the northwestern Wisconsin map roads, Burt summarized his journeys with me with this comment: "I'll go half a mile to see something scenic."

Ten Things I Now Know about Wisconsin's North Woods

This book is divided into six sections, and while each section is unique, several common themes and impressions tie them all together.

1. It's hard to disconnect from the North Woods. Wherever I went I met many residents who had migrated to the area because, as visitors, they just couldn't get its beauty and peacefulness out of their minds. So they pulled up stakes wherever they were and moved north. Several were in the inn and restaurant business, like the Moldenhauers in Spread Eagle, who own The Lodge at River's Edge, and Irma Hicks in Fifield, who owns Hicks Landing. These folks began their love affair with the north country via vacations, then felt permanently drawn to the area's forests and lakes.

2. The North Woods hosts a lot of odd and unusual festivals. Take the Flambeau Rama in Park Falls, which includes a frog-jumping contest, Rutabaga Fest in Cumberland, which celebrates rutabagas, the Great Hodag Duck Chase Festival in Rhinelander, and the Turtle Lake festival, hosting, of course, turtle races.

3. North Woods folks love outlandish memorials. There's that mammoth loon in Mercer announcing the town's status as the state's Loon Capital, the enormous walk-through muskie in Hayward, the larger-than-life deer in the front of the Northwoods Supper Club in Fifield, and, of course, the gargantuan Paul Bunyan at the Cook Shanty Restaurant in Minocqua.

4. Things have changed from the fishing lodge heyday in the 1930s and 1940s. The North Woods has a huge variety of accommodations, ranging from cottages and campgrounds, to inns, bed and breakfasts and resorts, to a fairly new type of accommodation—the vacation home. The way in which people vacation has changed too. Long ago, visitors would come for weeks, even months, at a time. But today, visitors don't have as much free time. Consequently, they often spend long weekends or perhaps a week at a time.

5. The North Woods is sprinkled with many fine old resorts and lodges still going strong. Take the Chanticleer Inn in Eagle River, Boyd's Mason Lake Resort in Fifield, of Ted Moody's Camp, now called Spider Lake Lodge Bed and Breakfast, in Hayward—they're all venerable northern institutions, and there are many more like them out there.

6. There are many good Jeopardy questions about the North Woods. Examples: Q. Where did Smoky Bear originate? A. Mercer.

Q. Where is Wisconsin's first state park? A. St. Croix Falls.

7. North Woods establishments love to show off fish. You'll see photos of locally caught fish plastered on counters of gas stations, convenience stores, restaurants, and taverns. You'll also see mounted fish (muskies are the favorite for showing off) decorating walls and ceilings throughout the region.

8. North Woods towns were settled by people who worked hard and played hard. That balance is still prevalent.

9. There's a sense of fantasy in the North Woods. When I saw a sign for pony rides outside a furniture store near Hayward, I thought it captured the essence of why so many people are attracted to Wisconsin's northern woods and waters. They offer a real chance to abandon your adult inhibitions and relive your childhood. It doesn't matter if you're in town or out in the woods, Wisconsin's northland offers up the chance to feel like you're at camp again.

10. Supper clubs are alive and well in the North Woods. They're a pervasive feature throughout the region. By and large, they serve excellent food complete with old-fashioned relish trays and lots of personal attention served up by the owner. I hope you'll find this guidebook helpful when you decide what you want to see and do in northern Wisconsin. This book was not intended to cover every nook and cranny in the state's northern counties; rather, it was put together to capture the highlights of an area. I hope I have not inadvertently left out information about your favorite haunt.

On Madison's Capitol Square, on May 29, 1998, Governor Tommy Thompson officially opened Wisconsin's Sesquicentennial festivities. I was there, ringing one of the commemorative bells celebrating the event. I was in the midst of working on this book and thought of the many wondrous things Wisconsin has accomplished in 150 years. The industries in the state's North Woods and their hard-working people have played an important role in shaping the state's history. This northern expanse of land has grown from being home to numerous lumber and mining boom towns to being a woodland, water, and wilderness playground like no other.

I am delighted to see that I have transferred my enthusiasm for northern Wisconsin to my three children, Siri, Nissa, and Sim. I hope you too will get caught up in the contagious spell of the region. To grab attention, there's an old newspaper admonition that urges writers to "get them in the tent." I hope I've been able to get you into the North Woods tent.

Warm regards for happy wandering.

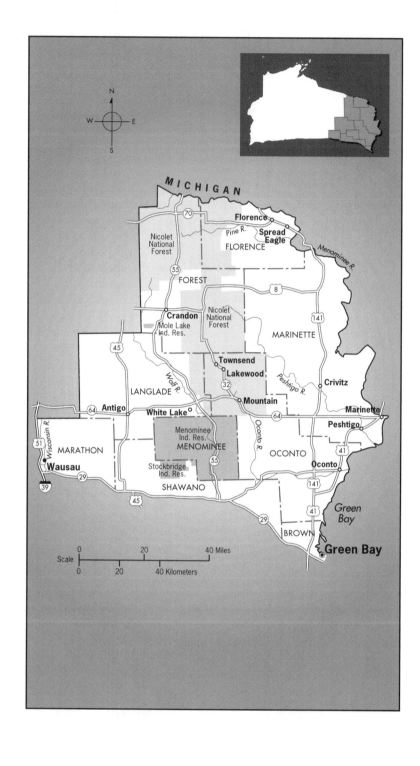

chapter 1
the Far Northeast

a t first glance, northeast Wisconsin seems almost too good to be true. This pocket of natural beauty is so abundant with deciduous forests, dense evergreen pine groves, dazzling lakes, rivers, and streams, it's easy to lose your heart to the land. An invisible outline of the section, frequently referred to as the North Woods, begins at Wausau, moves northeast to the edge of the Wisconsin-Upper Michigan border, turns southeast along this boundary all the way to Marinette, then edges along U.S. Highway 29 through Shawano, and back again to Wausau.

In the interior of this irregular circle is the magnificent Nicolet National Forest. This epic gem of incredible magnitude (some 661,000 acres) draws visitors to its towering forests with trees as old as 400 years. Year-round visitors hike, bike, camp, or ski in the forest's three wilderness areas. The Nicolet, pronounced "nick-oh-LAY," is the epitome of a North Woods wilderness escape. Looking to make your way through the forest on water? A smorgasbord of opportunities is waiting. Over 1,200 lakes are yours for the choosing.

Another element distinguishing the northeast is the moody Wolf River, a federally designated wild river that easily lives up to its restless reputation. A favorite with rafters and canoeists, the Wolf begins a rambling descent northeast of Antigo at its headwaters in Lily, then meanders south, eventually joining the lower Fox River system and Lake Winnebago. Along the way the river's character frequently changes. It's that transition on short notice, from serene water to white-water roller coaster, that causes hearts to pound and thrill seekers to feel right at home. Those who yearn for excitement relish the Wolf at its snarliest as it plummets nearly 1,000 feet, churning through canyons of the Menominee Reservation near Shawano.

What else sets the northeast apart from other areas of Wisconsin? Simply put, it's one of the best kept secrets around. If you want solitude surrounded by forests, lakes, streams, and an astonishing array of flora and fauna, you've got it. Northeast Wisconsin is where you can almost hear the vegetation growing—music to city dwellers' ears. This is a wonderful place to do nothing but stretch out in a hammock and ponder the views. No wonder those who live here are determined to keep it as ruggedly pristine as when they arrived. You too may feel the way local townsfolk do—that you are the first to put down footprints on your own staked-out territory.

It's that unspoiled seclusion that is at the heart of the northeast's magic. If you've overlooked this area, you're not alone. Northeast Wisconsin is often referred to as 'the most secretive' of Wisconsin's best-kept secrets. Don't be surprised if you never see another soul while exploring logging, hiking, and ski trails. More surprisingly, you can drive for miles on main highways and often not see another car pass in either direction. This land of mighty pines, wild rivers, and splendid waterfalls is my personal favorite for 'best of the most isolated places in the state.' Getting close to nature is a snap, and if you want to get lost for a while, that's easy too. In the past, the feeling seemed to be that if you ventured to northeast Wisconsin you were undoubtedly an adventuresome traveler. While still considered remote by many who seek the ultimate North Woods experience, that attitude is changing as more visitors discover the stirring beauty of this underdeveloped land.

Typical of the back-to-nature experiences abundantly available in the northeastern woods is the three-hour Family Fun Rafting Adventure at Bob's Rafts in Langlade. After only a few minutes of paddling on the Wolf River and before going through the first set of rapids, my companion and I were treated to our first waterfront wildlife sighting. A newborn fawn came into view, straddling the rocks in an attempt to traverse the shallow riverbed. I was tempted to get out of the raft and push the deer along; I was that close, but I resisted the temptation. Later, after conquering three invigorating sets of rapids, we spotted a fast-moving face swimming close to the raft. It was an energetic brown beaver offering the comic relief we needed after working the river. In its mouth, a voluminous bouquet of long-stemmed purple flowers.

For sheer underexplored, rustic beauty, northeast Wisconsin takes the blue ribbon. For those longing for the ultimate North Woods experience, without the tourists, it's a mandatory stop.

Antigo

Near Antigo, travelers unfamiliar with the area might wonder why so many fields have slatted wooden roofs. The reason is ginseng, a crop that grows only in the shade. Wisconsin dominates the world production of this root, then exports it to the Orient for use as a medicinal herb. Wisconsin soil is also famous for something else that is abundant around Antigo. The next time you come this way, consider one reason Antigo has earned a place on the map. That reason is silt loam—Wisconsin's official state soil, and the main reason potato farming thrives in this environment.

On your way Up North, take time to look around the town's nooks and crannies from yesteryear. On quick inspection, it's easy to discern that the community is proud of its roots. Ask a resident for interesting sites to visit, and the response might be to inspect the formal Colonial Building, constructed in 1905 at 404 Superior Street, which now houses the Antigo Public Library.

And behind it is another spot often mentioned as not to be missed. The 1878 small log house on the library lawn is the original home of Antigo's founder, Francis Deleglise. Both properties are listed on the National Register of Historic Places. Deleglise named the town for Spring River (*Nequi-Antiog-Seebah*, a Chippewa word), which weaves its way through the area.

Antigo, a wide expanse of landscape located on a plateau (also known as the Antigo Flats), once attracted a drove of settlers because of its superb soil and local lumbering. The river channels in the area were used to float logs downstream, via the Wolf River to Shawano, Oshkosh, and Wausau.

Antigo recognizes the importance of preserving its past. Its downtown has over 200 businesses and specialty shops, many of which are housed in renovated buildings. I drove through Antigo many times, often passing the large turreted blue building in the middle of downtown, at 737 5th Avenue and at the corner of Clermont Street. Each time I passed by I wondered about its history. Eventually, my curiosity got the better of me, and I entered the Vosmek Drug Store with the feeling that this architectural marvel had many stories within its walls. I wasn't disappointed.

Pat Frey, owner of the drugstore, took time to peruse the building's archives and give me a tour of the past. Starting out as the site of the City Drug Store in 1899, the building has been home to several businesses, but the first floor has been used mainly as a drugstore during its long history. In 1940 the business changed hands when George Vosmek, a graduate of the University of Wisconsin School of Pharmacy, bought it and put his name over the door. Thirty-six years later Vosmek retired, and Pat Frey took over the helm of running Antigo's long-established pharmacy.

While commercial business was going on within the walls of the first floor, other interesting developments were taking place above it. In 1882, five years after Deleglise founded Antigo, the Lodge of the International Order of Odd Fellows was established. When the building was built in 1888, the Odd Fellows found a home for their activities. Antigo residents with a long memory recall the Vosmek building as being the site of the glory years of a grand old lodge. A splendid ballroom on the second floor, open to the public, was the centerpiece of this grandeur. The 60-foot hall had golden-oak moldings, elaborate Brussels carpeting, and, at the height of its splendor, a magnificent ceiling dome with over 160 incandescent electric bulbs. The spacious hall eventually fell into disrepair and has not been used since the early 1940s, but memories of the elaborate ballroom and music by the Antigo City Orchestra live on among the city elders.

There is something else intriguing about the building. You can view a human skull on a back shelf with several news clipping attached. In 1939, a colorful local fellow from nearby Lily known as Patches was murdered, and his remains were found in a field outside Antigo. Pat Frey's grandfather, John Smith, was sheriff at the time, and Patches's skull, which was used as evidence in the well-known murder trial, came into his possession.

Visitors to Antigo today do more than visit the downtown. They come to fish for muskie, panfish, trout, and walleye in the abundant streams, rivers, and lakes in the area. Two golf courses are also close by: Riverview, 5 miles west of town and Antigo Bass Lake, 18 miles north. Within the city's 47 acres of parks many fine hiking and biking trails are available.

Sights and Attractions

Deleglise Cabin. When you drive by the library you'll see an old log structure on the lawn. This small, antiquated cabin is Antigo's first home. Open limited hours from late May to late August. 404 Superior Street. (715) 627-4464.

Langlade County Historical Museum. Historical artifacts and oddities from Langlade County's history. In 1998, the museum moved to the Old Carnegie Library Building, 404 Superior Street. (715) 627-4464.

Mole Lake Casinos. Reel slots, wheel of fortune, blackjack, and more. Weekend entertainment. Need a place to stay? The casinos run Mole Lake Motel, a pleasant spot three blocks from the gambling action. The casinos are located 32 miles northeast of Antigo on WI 55, in Mole Lake. (800) 236-WINN or (715) 478-5770.

The home of Mepps fishing lures, near the intersection of Highways 64 and 45 in Antigo. The huge plant is a favorite stop of anglers and curious visitors, who get behind-the-scenes knowledge of fishing gear production during guided tours.

Sheldon's, Inc. This is the home of Mepps fishing lures. Take a guided tour of the plant and trophy room. A must for any angler or for those curious about how fishing lures are made. Antigo. 626 Center Street. (715) 623-2382.

Events

Music in The Park. The place to be on Monday nights from early June to the end of August is the Antigo City Park Bandstand. Old-fashioned ice cream socials and 'to-die-for' pies accompany the music, which starts at 7 p.m.

Off-Road Championships. This annual gathering of hot wheels, at the Langlade County Fairgrounds in Antigo, is recognized nationally as an exciting event. It's often covered by ESPN television.

Snowshoe Rendezvous. Annual January snowshoe extravaganza celebrates snowshoeing as you've never seen it. Snowshoe events, races, workshops, and demonstrations at the Bear Paw Inn.

Triple 'R' Riding Club Horse Show. This annual mid-July horse show has been going strong since the early 1950s. Pleasure and speed events—something for everyone. Langlade County Fairgrounds Horse Arena.

For more information about these and other events contact the Antigo Chamber of Commerce, (715) 623-4134.

Lodging

Cutlass Motor Lodge. Indoor pool, dining room, weekend packages. Not far from the Langlade County Fairgrounds. 915 S. Superior Street, U.S. 45 South. (800) 288-5277 or (715) 623-4185.

Rollingstone Lake Resort. Cottages and campsites on picturesque Rollingstone Lake. Fishing boats and paddleboats available for rent. W10650 Bass Lake Road, Deerbrook. (715) 484-5211.

Twin Oaks Resort. House-keeping cottages with a boat to boot. Open year-round. A snowmobile paradise—trails start at your door. N10870 Circle Drive, Elcho. (715) 275-3917.

Out to Eat

Antigo Bass Lake Country Club. The public is welcome at this 18-hole golf course, plus restaurant and lounge. 18 miles north of Antigo. W10650 Bass Lake Road, Deerbrook. (715) 623-6201.

Blackjack Steak House. Char-broiled steaks, chicken, and prime rib are house specialties. They cook up a mean Friday night seafood buffet. 800 S. Superior Street. (715) 623-2514.

Cheers Restaurant and Lounge. Open for breakfast, lunch, and dinner. A

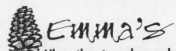

Emma's

Like other travelers, when I'm on the road I often stop for nourishment and conversation. Anyone who wants to start a northern jaunt on the right foot stops at Emma Krumbee's for morning soul food. Emma's, located at Exit 190, off U.S. 51 in Wausau, is an offshoot of the 'mother store' in Belle Plain, Minnesota.

If good coffee and bakery goods sound like staples of a good trip, then you have reasons aplenty to take in the pervasive country atmosphere here. On my first visit I consumed one of Emma's gooey dinner-plate-sized cinnamon rolls, then fought off guilt feelings all the way to Antigo. Not anymore. Now, I purposely put guilt aside and use Emma's as an excuse to begin a northern adventure.

All trips have to start somewhere, so, why not roll out from someplace where you feel astonishingly good.

popular place, locals like the pizza and salad bar. At the corner of one of the town's main intersections—U.S. 45 and WI 64. (715) 623-2249.

Gunkel's Bakery. A bakery so popular they put in a drive-through window. When was the last time you saw that at a bakery? Great breads and pastries-take home their unusual flax seed bread. 231 Superior Street. (715) 623-4019.

Hill's Still. A favorite gathering spot on Friday and Saturday nights. Supper club with a wilderness touch. The chicken, fish, and prime rib are big hits with regulars. Five miles south of Mole Lake Casino. (715) 484-3211.

Shopping

Country Corner. Wander through a Christmas barn and shop for goodies like Wisconsin maple syrup. 734 S. Superior Street. (715) 623-3429.

Jaclyn M. Schroeder's Art Gallery & Gifts. Array of artistic items. Nice selection of art and gifts. 710 S. Superior Street. (715) 623-4150.

Nicolet National Forest

There are many impressive facts about the Nicolet, the most staggering of which is its size. In 1632 French explorer Jean Nicolet first came upon the area which was part of a territory called the 'eastern shore.' Nicolet also explored the area where Green Bay, Wisconsin's oldest community, is located, as well as the woods and waters north of Lake Michigan's shores. Today, in Nicolet's honor, a mammoth 661,000 acres have been set aside as the Nicolet National Forest, a territory so big it comes close to matching the size of Rhode Island.

Statistics about this underexplored area are as impressive as its size. The Nicolet includes 1,170 lakes, 580 miles of trout steams, 3,600 miles of back roads, and 450 miles of snowmobile trails. Sixty-eight species of fish, deer, bobcats, wild turkey, and a black bear for every four square miles typify the area's abundant wildlife. There are also 960 plant species within the boundaries of the Nicolet—another fascinating fact about this North Woods wonder.

Jean Nicolet would probably be surprised to learn that the area with his name on it is still predominately unexplored. This hauntingly beautiful backdrop is unparalleled for hiking, boating, canoeing, fly-fishing, rafting, cross-country skiing, and snowshoeing. The area is so breathtaking, it regularly draws photographers and outdoor enthusiasts throughout the four seasons. It's also a berry-picking paradise. The Nicolet is home to tons of blueberries, blackberries, and raspberries, free for the picking. Words to the wise: Choose one section of the Nicolet, then explore it one trek at a time.

The area is so big it is divided into four districts: Florence, Lakewood, Laona, and Eagle River. Ranger stations in each district offer complimentary maps and handouts, as well as USGS topographical maps for a small fee. **Contact the Nicolet's headquarters in Rhinelander, (715) 362-1300, for additional information.**

You'll get your first glance of the Nicolet if you're traveling east, along WI 64 out of Antigo. For information about the Lakewood district of the Nicolet, continue on WI 64 through Langlade and then turn north on WI 32. **A quarter of a mile south of Lakewood you'll find the Lakewood Ranger Station, (715) 476-6333.** This resource center, a must stop for hikers, campers, or backpackers, has information about the forest's 22 developed campsites and hundreds of other rustic camping spots. The latter, called 'dispersed campsites,' usually aren't equipped with toilets or drinking water, but the trade-off is that you'll usually have the serene beauty of the backwoods all to yourself.

Wherever you are in the Nicolet, you'll have a good viewing area to watch the wondrous wildlife activity. As dusk turns into darkness, sit beside one of the forest's many lakes. You'll hear the night sounds of birds, insects, bats, and perhaps the high-pitched crooning of a coyote—backdrops to the ebb and flow of the waves. Eagles, loons, great blue herons, and songbirds also fill the air with their special sounds. At your feet, frogs of many sizes and colors curiously investigate your perch.

Hiking enthusiasts find that the Nicolet offers so many choices the difficulty is deciding which trail to start on first. The possibilities are nearly endless: over 800 miles of hiking, biking, and skiing trails to choose from. One of the best known is the Ice Age Trail, which traces the four glacial epochs that swept through the state thousands of years ago. The Ice Age Trail traces the paths of glaciers as it makes switchbacks from the state's northern forests to the southern part of the state, over 1,200 miles in all. About half of the trail, about 600 miles, has been established as the Ice Age National Scenic Trail. Sections of the Ice Age meander through the Nicolet—check the maps at the ranger station for specific locations. Whether you hike the Ice Age or a few of the Nicolet's other trails, don't be surprised if you come out of the woods wanting to hike them all.

the Wolf River

The Wolf River starts out as a trickle 25 miles below the Michigan state line, then flows 223 miles to Lake Winnebago. In Langlade County, it cuts through spectacular and rugged glacial terrain. Its Class II and Class III white-water rapids (there are 17 named rapids in Langlade County) are legendary and a hypnotic draw for those eager to experience uninhabited wilderness. For those who want the Wolf to propel them to this territory, a canoe, raft, or kayak is a perfect way to get there.

The Wolf has a reputation for being wild and unpredictable, but its moods also include a serene side. As the river winds its way south from northern Langlade County, above County T, it changes from a quiet stream in to a dramatic, rushing presence.

Those who live and work in this area know the Wolf well. For that reason, you should talk to local outfitters before you rent equipment. The level of the river dictates how early and how late the outfitters operate, but most are open from May through early October. Ask about the river's water level during your visit because its level can change daily. In late spring, the river is often the highest because of the run-off of melting snow. On the other hand, in late summer, the river may be shallow, with some sections only a few inches deep.

Never let your guard down though, because up ahead, another set of rapids is invariably waiting. Some sections of the river require you to be an expert canoeist. Ask a local outfitter what level of experience you need for specific areas of the river. Even if the river is shallow, maneuvering through rapids and rocks takes effort. However, if you get tired you always have the option of getting out and portaging your raft beyond the rapids.

Since the Wolf changes its personality so many times during its course of travel, there are sections that are probably just right for canoeists with various navigational skills. For example, if you paddle south from the Wild Wolf Inn in Langlade, you would come across 11 sections of water cutting through the landscape. The course includes steep runs, great challenges, and relative-

The wild Wolf River makes its way around massive boulders.

ly quiet open water. While the Wolf is an excellent whitewater river, it is known to be unpredictable. For that reason always wear your life jacket and rent equipment from a reputable outfitter.

In addition to white-water rafting, the Wolf also attracts all levels of trout fishing enthusiasts. If you like fly-fishing, this is your chance to stake your claim. A segment of the Wolf is devoted to your sport below Hollister and the Highway 64 bridge in Langlade. This portion of the river is one of Wisconsin's unique fly-fishing-only areas.

Several outfitters in the area rent rafting packages, which include rafts (most have a two-person minimum on board), paddles, life vests, and shuttle service to the river. Some rent only the equipment, others organize trips varying from all-day ventures to ones two to three hours in length. Here are some outfitters close to the Wolf.

Buettner's Wild Wolf Inn. In Langlade. Rents rafts (as well as fishing and cross-country ski gear) but does not offer organized river trips. (715) 882-8611.

Bob's Rafts. Shuttle service and several river trips of varying lengths are available. Use the changing room at Bob and Joni's Northern Lights Restaurant next door. At the intersection of WI 64 and WI 55 in Langlade. (715) 882-8304.

Herb's Raft Rental. Shuttle service and changing room; the minimum age for people renting equipment is 12. White Lake. (715) 882-8612.

Shotgun Eddy. Various runs, 4-10 foot waterfalls. A favorite spot to rent gear for those heading to Great Smoky Falls on the Menominee Reservation. (715) 882-4461.

Big Smoky Falls Rafting. Trip has three runs between the County WW bridge and three falls along the picturesque Wolf River Dells. The wild and woolly section at the end is the scariest. On the Menominee Reservation, south of Langlade and north of Shawano.

Closeby are the towns of White Lake, Mountain, Lakewood, and Townsend. At the heart of this area, they provide an Up North experience that is unforgettable and uncrowded, the year-round.

White Lake

Twenty miles east of Antigo, in eastern Langlade County, the sleepy town of White Lake is being rediscovered. This pocket of woods off the beaten track is home to one of the county's 418 lakes, the town's main attraction in the summer. Drive along the curving main road toward the village center and you're rewarded by lush green forests at the edge of shimmering White Lake. This is paradise for swimmers and boaters who remember what the old swimming hole was like. White Lake has a small sandy beach and an anchored raft offshore for those who want view the landscape from the water.

Visitors have begun to swing by here not only to take in the 'lake-in-the-woods' views but also to glimpse at nostalgia, North Woods style. From the late 1880s, when White Lake was settled, through the early 1900s, the town boomed as a mill and railroad community. In fact, it sprang up practically overnight because the mill and lumber companies had to have roots for their employees. White Lake does have a 'built-in-a-hurry' look but is not without charm. Oddly, the original houses are nearly identical to one another. To accommodate the isolated workers, a series of look-alike buildings were constructed, including a clubhouse, bank, barbershop, and rooming house. At the heart of this instant town, the picturesque Wisconsin and Northern ('Whiskey Northern') Railroad depot saw plenty of activity. Today, visitors can still view the depot, which is now a museum, thanks to the local histori-cal society. The structure was renovated and opened to the public in 1997.

But the main reason to poke around the town is to see its turn-of-the-cen-tury look-alike houses. Many are still in excellent condition and continue to give White Lake its characteristic old-time lumber town look.

Mountain

You won't find a mountain in Mountain, a quiet town frequently referred to as the Gateway to the North. Instead, you'll find rolling hills, scenic hik-ing, and snowmobile trails, along with a noteworthy spot for picnicking. If you're camping or hiking in the area, make sure you stop to pick up supplies at an emporium full of nostalgia but still going strong. This is Mountain Groceries, a huge old-fashioned general store and grocery with wooden floors, high ceilings, and friendly folk. Bulk items, typical grocery products, and a bit of the unusual, including make-your-own root beer powders and pickling spices, give this emporium a special character.

Mountain Grocery—Mountain's cavernous old-fashioned grocery store.

If heights don't bother you, climb to the top of the last remaining fire tower standing on its original site in the Nicolet National Forest (out of the original 19). Erected in 1934, it is on the National Registry of Historic Look-outs. To get to the tower, with its great views of the surrounding forest, go east from Mountain, turn onto County W, then travel on old WI 32 for about two and a half miles.

For those preferring to stay close to the ground, head south of Mountain for two miles, then, upon entering Nicolet National Forest, look for signs for Green Lake Park off WI 32 and WI 64. Here, on the southwest shore of crystal-clear Green Lake, you'll find a good place to stop and unwind. A comfortable log shelter, built by the U.S. Forest Service in 1937, offers an indoor fireplace and picnic tables.

Lakewood

Lakewood's claim to fame is its geographical location. The town's gateway position offers great access to prime woods and water destinations. Not only does Lakewood have the distinct privilege of being nestled among the expansive woods of the Nicolet National Forest it is also within a short drive of the Wolf and Peshtigo Rivers and over 60 superior fishing lakes. It's because of these natural resources that outdoor enthusiasts lured to the area swell the tiny town of a few hundred residents to three times its size in summer and fall.

Even if you're not into camping, hiking, or fishing, Lakewood is a good place to stop along the well-traveled Highway 32 corridor. Expect to find locals who enjoy voicing their concern for the changing landscape. Because of Lakewood's position on this popular north-south travel route, it's inevitable that the town is vulnerable to change.

In fact, signs of building and renovation along the town's main street are evident. You'll find new and old buildings clustered together on both sides of Highway 32 for several blocks. A word to those who like to take with

Cathedral Pines—400-year-old pine forest near Lakewood.

them the feeling of having "been there, done that": Lakewood has a cornucopia of boutiques featuring the popular "Up North" saying on a variety of sports clothes.

Townsend

Five minutes up the road from Lakewood is Townsend, home to about 700 year-round residents. Built along Military Road in 1864, the town was first named Johnson Siding, but that was before a Mr. Townsend hammered the first spike into the area's first railroad tie. Maybe Townsend's fellow workers wanted to reward him (the reason isn't clear) but they ended up naming this lonely outpost after him.

If you missed stopping at Lakewood for shopping and supplies, you'll find that Townsend has bait and sporting goods outlets, and a few gift shops (all peculiarly arranged on one side of the street), but many seasoned travelers come here because this is the place to stop and eat. Several restaurants, ranging from small diners to supper clubs, serve a wide range of good food, including seafood buffets and down-home, hearty country breakfasts.

Sights and Attractions

Cathedral of Pines. This area four miles west of Lakewood is not easy to find, but once you do, you'll understand why it's been called one of the most impressive pine forests in the United States. It is also all that is left of Oconto County's virgin pines. As the story goes, the pines were saved because the wife of the owner of a logging company persuaded her husband to spare the mighty pines from the inevitable logging saw. North of Lakewood, on WI 32, look for a sign on your left, then turn west on Archibald Lake Road. The road twists for about four miles through a deeply canopied forest. When you come to a sign for Cathedral Drive, make a sharp right. Drive about a mile on a narrow, bumpy road until you see the sign "Welcome To Cathedral of Pines."

Acquired by the Forest Service in the 1990s, the land is comprised of vir-

Doorway to Holt Balcolm Logging Camp.

gin white and red pines believed to be about 400 years old. Towering hemlocks and hardwoods add beauty to the ancient wilderness. Visitors often describe a visit here as being not unlike a spiritual experience. Whatever you absorb from your experience, you'll undoubtedly remember how small you felt as you walked beneath the giant trees in this mystical forest.

The Cathedral of Pines is also a nesting area for the great blue heron. Over 100 nesting pairs are usually found in the area. If you spot a rookery, don't startle the birds. Forest rangers advise hikers to stay at least 300 feet away from these nesting birds.

Holt Balcolm Logging Camp. Here you'll see how progress has not gotten in the way of history. The Holt Balcolm Logging Camp, off County F, south of Lakewood, is easy to find if you're also looking for Lakewood's challenging 18-hole McCauslin Brook Golf and Country Club. Wisconsin's oldest logging camp, and the oldest camp of its kind in the country, is located in the middle of the golf course. The setting is also interesting since the old logging camp is not far from a 2,600-foot grass airstrip.

Drive south of Lakewood on WI 32, then follow County F to the golf course. When you enter the grounds, park at the first parking lot. Built in 1880, the log cookhouse offers a logger's view of what it must have been like

A Few Favorites

Favorite View. A great gazing spot for taking in the serene side of the Wolf River is from an overstuffed couch on the comfortable enclosed porch of the Wolf River Lodge. The lodge is high on a bluff overlooking the river, and from this vantage point you'll see a profusion of huge boulders dramatically punctuating the clear water and its occasional feathery white rapids.

Favorite Drive. About a mile after leaving the intersection of WI 55 and WI 64 in Langlade, drive east into the Nicolet National Forest. For about 15 miles, this stretch of highway is bordered with splendid pines and firs, trees so tall the land has a whimsical Jack-and-the-Beanstalk feel to it. A good time to take in this mighty country is autumn, when the landscape is transformed into a blazing palette of color. Keep your eyes open and you might spot a bear, as I did one late July afternoon as it jaunted across the highway.

Favorite Outing. Wisconsin's northeast woods and waters are good places to swim, boat, fish, hike, bike, or play golf, but for many who descend upon this giant outdoor playground the lure is white-water rafting. If you've never done it, try it. If you think rafting is just for those who like to live dangerously, think again. Wolf River adventurers have Class II and Class III rapids to duel with, but there are plenty of good spots for easy family rafting. A favorite place to raft is the section of the Wolf between Irrigation Hole and Langlade. In late summer it's often slow-moving and suitable for taking children along. It has a good mix of rapids (three sets) and placid water. And it only takes a maximum of three hours to navigate. For visitors with little time and not much rafting experience, this is an ideal outing. Nearby, you'll find Bob's Rafts in Langlade. For easy, fun rafting, sign up for the Family Fun Rafting Adventure. Make sure to wear life preservers!!

to dine on blue-and-white-speckled tinware at a rustic log table. Restored by the McCauslin Lions Club, the logging camp is open from June through September. (715) 276-7561 or Lakewood Area Chamber of Commerce, (715) 276-6500.

Woodland Trail Winery. Set in a woodsy location at the intersection of Big Hill Road and WI 32 in Lakewood, the Woodland Trail Winery specializes in making wine from regional cherries, apples, cranberries, and grapes, producing more than 40 different types of wine each year. Complimentary wine tasting and winery tours are offered. All wines made on location are featured in the retail shop. If you're looking for a made-in-Wisconsin product, these wines make unique gifts. (715) 276-3668.

The Langlade Fish Hatchery. Each year, the Department of Natural Resources raises over 200,000 German brown trout at this facility. Something else of interest—about six million suckers are raised annually as food for muskies. (715) 882-8757.

Gingerbread Houses. Most visitors don't stumble upon these quaint creations, they purposely go looking for them. In the early 1930s, Wilmot Swanson began building his first storybook house from cobblestones, wood, and stone, all taken from his property at **Camp Lake Resort**. The result was Rock Cottage, an imaginative structure often referred to as "folk art architecture." Rock Rest, another marvel, came next. His most elaborate work, Gingerbread House (which lends its name to the entire complex), was built last. It's a Hansel-and-Gretel cottage that looks as if it were fashioned out of gingerbread, hand-baked, then decorated with candy and icing.

Raft preparation at Great Smoky Falls.

All three cottages, along with several log cabins, are part of Camp Lake Resort. Swanson's cottages are marvelous tributes to one person's devotion to whimsy and design, but when you realize he worked alone, often from daybreak to sunset, gathering, selecting, and moving thousands of cobblestones, the feat becomes difficult to imagine. There was another thing Swanson did that was unusual. He created all of his buildings from ideas in his head—he never used any blueprints or construction drawings.

All five fairy-tale-like cottages are privately owned, so you can view them only from the road. However, several other Camp Lake cottages are available to rent. Contact John and Esther Larson (Esther is Swanson's daughter) at 15867 Tree Farm Road, Mountain, 54149, or phone (715) 276-6431. To see the houses, follow WI 32 north from Mountain for five miles, turn left on North Maiden Lake Road (Forest Road 2295), then follow it for three miles.

Great Smoky Falls and Dells of the Wolf River. The spectacular Great Smoky Falls are part of the Menominee Nation Reservation. As you travel through the reservation, watch for a sign pointing west to the falls. There are two outstanding natural attractions in this area, and a fork in the road should help you decide which one to see first. If you take the road to the right side of the fork, you'll come to a lovely river walk called the Dells of the Wolf River. Even though you might question the wisdom of exploring private land, you'll soon discover that members of the Menominee Nation welcome you to their rocky cliffs above the Wolf River. For a small fee you can explore the waterside trails and see the Wolf from a lofty perspective. Back at the fork in the road, take the left turn and you'll come to a parking area adjacent to the Wolf River. For another small fee you'll navigate a crude bridge that takes you to where excitement reigns supreme. Below the cliffs, the falls boom snowy white cascading water.

From late spring to mid-autumn, blue rubber rafts, paddled by rafters in orange life vests, dot the landscape. For sheer pleasure, this spot of the Wolf River is the pinnacle of a river rafting adventure. If you like challenges, you might want to forego your spectator position at the railing and rent a raft

Rafting the spectacular Great Smoky Falls.

upstream from one of the many outfitters in the area. Be sure to check conditions and wear a life preserver.

Camp 5 Lumberjack Museum and Steam Train. Twenty miles north of Townsend, explore history and the scenic North Woods by riding the Lumberjack Special steam train. The Camp 5 logging compound, listed on the National Register of Historic Places, features a nature center, logging museum, blacksmith shop, and many activities, including a forest tour. The steam train runs mid-June to late August. Closed Sundays. Saturday tours are for fall color viewing. At U.S. 8 and WI 32, Laona. (800) 774-3414.

Lodging

LAKEWOOD

Waubee Lodge Resort and Supper Club. Located on picturesque Waubee Lake in the heart of the Nicolet, the 140-acre waterfront setting is a favorite family vacation spot. Lakefront cabins have fireplaces and great views. (715) 276-6091.

MOUNTAIN

Winter Green. A charming country bed and breakfast inn surrounded by a 100-year-old forest of spruce, maple, and pine. Situated within the Nicolet National Forest, the inn also borders the Oconto County Recreational Trail. A good place to relax and enjoy the outdoors. (715) 276-6885.

TOWNSEND

Water's Edge Cottages. On Lake Archibald. Year-round waterfront cottages with kitchens and two and three bedrooms. This cozy shoreline retreat is located in one of the most unspoiled areas of the Nicolet National Forest. (715) 276-7628.

WHITE LAKE

Bear Paw Inn. More than just a place to stay (cabins, campsites, and bed and breakfast are available), you can also rent skis, snowshoes, mountain bikes, and rafts at this one-stop "outdoor education center." (715) 882-3502

Buettner's Wild Wolf Inn. Overlooks the Wolf River in Langlade, about three miles from White Lake. Three guest houses are also available for rent at

Historic Wolf River Lodge near Langlade.

Buettner's Motel. (715) 882-2186

Loggers Hotel. The name itself might inspire you to stop. Small inn exudes local charm. 634 Bissell Street. (715) 882-3471.

Wild Wolf Inn. Small inn close to the Nicolet, snowmobile, and cross-country ski trails. Breakfast, lunch, and dinner served daily. N2580 WI Highway 55. (715) 882-8611.

Wolf River Lodge. This historic lodge was built in 1919 from native hemlock logs, then rebuilt in 1929 after a fire. The welcome mat is out. Your name is written on a small blackboard in the front parlor. Braided rugs, antiques, quilts, and memorabilia galore. Full breakfast includes the lodge's famous crepes with "Eskimo jam." (715) 882-2182.

Out to Eat
LAKEWOOD

Maiden Lake Supper Club. A favorite gathering spot of locals, the club serves mouth-watering walleye, Black Angus steaks, prime rib, and assorted fish nightly from 5 p.m. Charm and character abound, from the rustic bar with fireplace, to the outdoor cocktail deck overlooking Maiden Lake. One mile south of Lakewood off WI 32, then one mile on Maiden Lake Road. (715) 276-6479.

Waubee Lodge Resort and Supper Club. Another popular spot to congregate, the restaurant features cocktail and karaoke bars and lakeside dining aside Nicolet's Waubee Lake. (715) 276-6091.

MOUNTAIN

Mountain Top Restaurant. Touted as having the "best Mexican food north of Green Bay and Appleton," this spot also features steaks and fish fries. Open year-round. Breakfast is served daily in summer and on weekends in the fall. Lunch and dinner served daily from 11 A.M. to 9 P.M. On WI 32. (715) 276-7233.

TOWNSEND

Old Town Hall. A favorite omelet stop located in Townsend's original town hall built in the 1920s. Breakfast is served from 5:30 A.M. Subs, soups, salads, sandwiches are also available. WI 32. (715) 276-3020.

Linssen's. Serves a breakfast buffet on Sunday, a seafood buffet on Friday night, and a Saturday night dinner buffet. Open seven days a week. WI 32. (715) 276-7539.

Rye's Hillcrest Lodge. Sandwiches, steaks, and shrimp on Saturday night, roast chicken on Sunday. Located a half mile west of WI 32 on Nicolet Road in Townsend. (715) 276-6772.

Shopping

One thing is for sure. If you like shopping, Lakewood has a nice mix of shops offering treasures such as exquisite handcrafted jewelry, silk and dried floral arrangements, and a variety of gifts and potpourri.

Chapel Antiques and Collectibles. North of town on WI 32, this shop houses a Christmas cottage as well as an interesting collection of gifts, antiques, and distinctive clothing. (715) 276-3590.

Decorative Doodles. Stock up on painting and stencil supplies or save time by purchasing gifts and accessories hand painted by artists. Across from the bank on WI 32. (May-Oct.)(715) 276-9889.

Hixon Creations. The mix here is the thing—gourmet coffee, unusual cards, and handcrafted specialties, including Yankee candles. On WI 32, one block south of County F. (715) 276-3024.

Nicolet Studio. You'll find original creations by Joan White, artist and owner of this working studio and gallery. A graduate of the School of the Art Institute of Chicago, White has exhibited her original work, consisting mostly of wildlife themes, throughout the Midwest. Shop for art, watch her paint, or engage in one of her favorite topics of conversation-preservation of wildlife. One block off WI 32 (behind Super Valu). (715) 276-6464.

Swede's Place. The variety is eclectic-toys, dolls, books, and more. A half mile north of downtown on WI 32. (715) 276-7321.

Florence and Spread Eagle

Residents of Florence County, at the top of northeastern Wisconsin and at the border of Upper Michigan, frequently refer to their home as the heart of wild rivers country. They're referring to the mystical Pine and Popple Rivers, protected waters that have been officially designated by the state as "wild rivers." These turbulent waterways aren't the only untamed natural resources in the area. North of Florence is the boundary water of the Menominee River, separating Wisconsin and Upper Michigan. Here, unleashed water begins its dramatic whirlwind by cascading from a 10-foot waterfall, then pouring into picturesque Piers Gorge. Even though stretches of the river flow silently, the Menominee is often called the wildest white water in the Midwest.

Florence County is also home to 49 trout streams and 110 lakes. If you like exploring an area that has a "last outpost" feeling, this is your sort of place. For further proof that the area remains remote and undeveloped, consider the fact that Florence County is one of two Wisconsin counties that have the distinction of not having one incorporated town.

Florence, the county seat for Florence County, has a small business district, including a sprinkling of restaurants and cafes, but the charm of the area is its rugged and remote feel, a lot like that of the TV show *Northern Exposure*. Try to imagine what life was like here in the logging and mining era of the late 1880s. Florence, named for the wife of the superintendent of the Chapin Mines, was once home to 40 taverns. Local lead mining and logging attracted hearty men from many parts of the country, including many from northern Europe. Most of the newcomers came without their families. A string of taverns cropped up to satisfy their loneliness and serve as community gathering spots. Today, local tales of mystery and intrigue abound regarding the men who worked the forests and mines. Old Man Mudge, a legendary local character, is purported to have kept a stockade of "necessary items" (including beautiful women) for the benefit of local laborers.

At the inviting Friend's and Visitor's Center in Florence, built in 1992, you can learn more about the area's history. It's a good place to inspire you to think about a variety of things. Things like why logging, at least the way it used to be carried out in the nineteenth century, eventually came to a end. The rush to strip the land was, as Stewart Udall pointed out in his book, *The Quiet Crisis*, a myth of superabundance. Visitors learn that commercial property needs to be well managed. In noncommercial areas, such as the Nicolet National Forest and county-owned forests, the land helps reduce run-off and adds a protected environment for vegetation and wildlife.

Still, the old-time logging industry is something to behold. At the Visitor's Center you'll see a "branded tree," one with a logger's initials carved in it, an example of how business was conducted in the logging industry's heyday. When logs were sent downstream to lumber mills, such primitive monograms offered proof of ownership. Look at the photo of the huge, indigenous king white pines, and it's easy to see how Florence-area trees played a role in rebuilding the city of Chicago after the fire of 1871.

There are many activities to pursue in the Florence and Spread Eagle area in all seasons of the year. But part of the reason to visit is to get to know the people who have settled here. Five miles down the road from Florence, on U.S. 2/141, is Spread Eagle, a place easy to miss if you're not looking but one with a name hard to forget. The town draws its name from early Native American settlers, who thought the area's chain of lakes looked similar to the spread shape of an eagle's wings.

Years ago John and Carol Moldenhauer, from Milwaukee, fell in love with the panoramic wilderness adjacent to the Menominee River in Spread Eagle. There they spent eight years building a rambling home on 10 acres of magnificent pines, one of which is believed to be between 200 and 300 years old. You too can enjoy the spectacle of the site because their home is also a bed and breakfast, appropriately named **The Lodge at River's Edge**.

Early one night, while talking to John Moldenhauer about area wildlife, I learned that six wild turkeys roosted in their pines each night. As if on cue, six enormous birds, three toms and three hens, strutted close to where we watched from the window. It was twilight when John explained the routine that would come next. Suddenly, each turkey taxied into position, then, with a running start, soared into the arms of the pines above. John said this was their way of shutting down and going to bed for the night. The remarkable ritual never varies, and, if you get up early, you can see the routine reversed at dawn. Big birds in big trees, quite a sight.

Later, in the dark, we walked a few yards down the wooden stairway to the edge of the Menominee River to practice wolf howling. Approximately 125 gray wolves live in the area, and when you call to them at night, sometimes they'll respond. If you don't get an answer, you can return during January and February for wolf-howling expeditions put on jointly by a biologist from the Department of Natural Resources, Northwoods Wilderness Outfitters, and The Lodge at River's Edge. Adventurers (no skills required) are taken by van, outfitted with snowshoes and headlamps, then guided to areas where wolves are known to be in the area.

If you're venturing off the beaten track in this region of northeastern Wisconsin, bring a map. The majestic waterfalls and spectacular forests are worth the effort of winding through the back roads, but it's easy to take a wrong turn and get lost. My motto: "Don't go anywhere that you can't back out of." But even if you do get lost, once you've poked around this corner of the state, you can't help but think the world is a more beautiful place than it was earlier in the day.

Sights and Attractions

Florence County Jail and Florence County Courthouse. The ebb and flow of commerce is gaining ground in Florence, but you know the past is alive and well when you ask a local resident to point out interesting sites and you're directed to the local jail. This structure, along with the courthouse, were built in 1889 and are listed on the National Register of Historic Places. The courthouse is an unusual example of Romanesque architecture. Both buildings offer exceptional opportunities for absorbing local history. One block south of U.S. 2, at 501 Lake Street. The jail is open to the public from Memorial Day through Labor Day.

Florence County Waterfalls. There are many spectacular waterfalls in the area, but seven are the most sought after: Meyers, Bull, Jennings, Big Bull, Little Bull, LaSalle, and Washburn. A significant amount of walking and hiking is necessary to get to all of the falls. Of these, LaSalle is the most breathtaking. It's located about eight miles southwest of Florence. Pick up a map at the Florence Natural Resources and Wild Rivers Interpretive Center (see next entry below) for the best route to get to the falls.

Florence Natural Resources and Wild Rivers Interpretive Center. Compact, worthwhile resource center (also considered the area's visitor center) where you can pick up useful maps, see wildlife exhibits, and glean historical information. Located at the intersection of U.S. 2 and WI 101/70. (715) 528-5377.

Pine and Popple Rivers. One of the area's most scenic views can be captured along the brilliant shorelines of these officially designated wild rivers in autumn. Mother Nature's mosaics are exceedingly bright along these shores. Sugar maples, aspen, yellow birch, silver and red maples, hemlock, and cedar light up the landscape when the temperatures begin to dip.

Skiing. Downhill enthusiasts take heart. South of Florence, on WI 101, Keyes Peak Ski Hill offers skiing for all levels of ability. (715) 528-3228.

Spread Eagle Barrens Natural Area. Most travelers enjoy scouting out places that are hard to find. I had this proven to me when, despite having a good map, I missed more than one turn into this enchanting sanctuary; but I didn't give up. Roads here seem to mysteriously disappear, then reappear to entice you to follow them to offbeat sites not known to mapmakers. Create your own adventure by exploring more than 4,000 acres of pine and rare grassland. Wildflowers put on first-rate seasonal shows. From the Spread Eagle area, take access roads from U.S. 2 and County N.

Events

Chili Ski-in. January hot chili and cool skiing along the Lauterman Cross Country Ski Trail, on WI 70, west of Florence in the Nicolet National Forest.

4th of July. Boat parades on Keyes Lake and the Eagle Chain of Lakes.

Water Ski Shows. Free performances every Wednesday and Sunday evening, from mid-June through mid-August. Bring a lawn chair or spread a blanket in Spread Eagle's Vagabond's Park for good viewing of daredevil water-skiers.

Lodging
FLORENCE

Forest Motel. Close to restaurant, parks, and historical sites. Route 2, Box 1109. (715) 528-4426.

Lakeside Bed and Breakfast. On the shores of dreamy Fisher Lake. Guest rooms are attractively furnished with antiques and Amish quilts. Exercise room, hot tub, and hearty breakfasts. 509 Furnace St. (715) 528-3259.

Larsons Bay Resort. One- and two-bedroom housekeeping cottages have fully equipped kitchenettes; fishing boats available. Route 2, Box 756. (715) 696-3332.

SPREAD EAGLE

The Lodge at River's Edge. (See pages 21–22.) Upper and lower great rooms available; splendid breakfasts served in contemporary retreat along the shores of the Menominee River. HC2, Box 244-6. (715) 696-3406.

Out to Eat
FLORENCE

Dina Mia. Homemade pizza just like your mother made it. Mexican and Italian choices. Downtown Florence. (715) 528-4760.

IRON MOUNTAIN, MICHIGAN (five minutes east of Spread Eagle)

Gleason's 1891. This beautiful 1891 building has housed many business-es over the years, including the original Woods Hotel, a bank, a Wells Fargo station, and, in the twentieth century, the Iron Mountain Fire Station. Photos of its historic past line the walls. Arched windows, plenty of atmosphere. Salads, pasta, pizza, seafood, and great steaks (I enjoyed the Sirloin Sizzler). Downtown Iron Mountain. (906) 779-5300.

Romagnoli's. Authentic Italian dishes that will make you wonder if you are in Europe. Ravioli, spaghetti, gnocchi, fettucine Alfredo. Steaks, chicken, and seafood available too. Combination plates are their specialty. North on U.S. 2. (906) 774-7300.

SPREAD EAGLE

The Eagle's Nest. Old timers around here remember this as a colorful center for local shenanigans. Today, it's a favorite gathering spot for diners seeking good Italian fare, steaks, and seafood. One half mile off U.S. 2. Look for signs on the highway. (715) 696-6646.

The Chuckwagon. Popular place, particularly on weekends. Great burgers in a comfy log building. The menu also includes sandwiches, soups, and a terrific Friday night fish fry. U.S. 2. (715) 696-6220.

Marinette County

The story of the Marinette-Crivitz-Peshtigo area is one linked to fur and lumbering. French Canadian voyageurs and fur traders plied these woods and waters in the late 1600s and continued their trade for a full century later. It is known, for instance, that Chappee, an Native American trader and representative of a fur company, settled in the Menominee area in 1796.

By the mid-1800s the area was experiencing rapid growth due to its booming economy. The sawmills could barely keep up with the demand for the area's white pine.

For more information contact Marinette County Tourism, 601 Marinette Avenue, P. O. Box 512, Marinette, 54143. (715) 735-6681, (800) 236-6681.

Two of the county's most spectacular sights are the Menominee and Peshtigo Rivers. If you're not a white-water rafting enthusiast (you may change your mind once you see the looks of exaltation on the faces of the many rafters who frequent the area), you may not know that the famous Rapids White Water section (the upper part) of the Peshtigo River has the longest stretch of continuous white water in the Midwest. This former logging "avenue" also has many gentle stretches perfect for novice canoers.

For those who can't get enough of white-water wild rides, you can't beat the mighty Menominee. Compared to most other rivers in the state, this is indeed "big water." In fact, know before you go that this is the most challenging white water in all the Midwest. The river plunges over a 10-foot waterfall, then takes its riders on a eye-popping spin through Piers Gorge and its canyon walls. Not for the faint of heart, the inexperienced, or those without professional guides. Here are some rafters and outfitters for both rivers.

Argosy Adventures Rafting. Professional river runners provide guided rafting trips on the Menominee. There's a changing facility and picnic area nearby. Box 22, Niagara, 54151. (715) 251-3886.

Kosir's Rapid Rafts. Professional river guides offer guided trips on the Peshtigo; equipment and gear also available. If you want to relax but stay close to the river, catch up on sleep at the riverfront cabins. Kosir's comfortable restaurant is also at hand. W14073 County C, Athelstane. (715) 757-3431.

Thornton's Raft Company Resort & Campground. Rafting gear and trips provided on the Peshtigo. Accommodations available at the resort or at campground and cottages. 12882 Parkway Rd., Box 216, Athelstane. (715) 757-3311.

Typical river running season for both the Peshtigo and Menominee Rivers is late April through September.

Crivitz

Crivitz is in a vacation area known as the Gateway to Wisconsin's Canadian Wilderness. The area has many resorts, campgrounds, and parks. Visitors come to explore the Peshtigo River, High Falls, Caldron Falls, Johnson Falls, Sandstone Flowages, Lake Noquebay, and Crooked Lake, all in the vicinity of Crivitz. Fishing is big business around here. The area boasts of having the highest concentration of trout streams in the state. **For more information on the area call (800) CRIVITZ or (715) 757-3253.**

Marinette

Marinette, 170 miles north of Milwaukee, is a busy port city located on Green Bay. Once known as the White Pine Capital of the world in its heyday, it was home to sawmills that lined both sides of the Menominee River. Today, the city's lively marina is known as a superb charter fishing area. Rainbow and brown trout, coho, and steelhead salmon are all abundant in these waters.

Peshtigo

Peshtigo is a charming small town that has yet to shake the memories of the horrific fire that devastated the area in 1871. It is regarded by some as the worst fire in American history. As a testimony to the town's steadfastness, early inhabitants who survived quickly initiated efforts to rebuild the town. The result is a thriving community with a fascinating museum (one block off U.S. 41) that tells its story.

Sights and Attractions

Crivitz Area Museum. Interesting museum traces the history of the area, from the early settlers, including Native Americans, lumbermen, and pioneers, to today's industries and businesses, including the growth of resorts and recreation. On South Street in Crivitz, at U.S. 41. Open May through September. (715) 854-3278.

Marinette County Historical Museum. The museum offers a fascinating look at the lumber and shipping industries, long prevalent in these parts.

Exhibits include models of Great Lakes schooners that transported milled lumber to Milwaukee and Chicago, a replica of a logging camp, and a log cabin from the 1800s. On Stephenson Island, off U.S. 41. Open June through September. (715) 732-0831.

Peshtigo Fire Museum. Although the Great Chicago Fire was devastating, the horrendous fire in Peshtigo on October 8, 1871, was far worse. Ironically, both fires occurred on the same day. Peshtigo's blaze goes down in history as the worst forest fire in the nation's history because hundreds of thousands of acres of timberland were lost. The town was also totally destroyed, and over 1,000 people lost their lives. The museum offers an intriguing look at this event. Open late May through early October. 400 Oconto Avenue. (715) 582-3244.

Waterfalls. Most visitors come to this area of the state to view waterfalls. Marinette County has several, but these 12, ranging from small, gentle falls to those with 18-foot drops, are the most spectacular: McClintock Falls in McClintock Park, Veteran's Falls in Veteran's Memorial Park, Strong Falls in Goodman Park, Twelve Foot Falls in Twelve Foot Falls Park, Horseshoe Falls, Eight Foot Falls in Twelve Foot Falls Park, Bull Falls, Dave's Falls in Dave's Falls Park, Long Slide Falls, Smalley Falls, Eighteen Foot Falls, and Piers Gorge. Most are located in the Marinette Park System. A small entrance fee is required.

Lodging
CRIVITZ

Paust's Woods Lake Resort. Something for everyone here. This popular spot, adjacent to the wild and woolly Caldron Falls Flowage, has been a North Woods magnet since 1900. Accommodations include a vacation-type motel, plus cottages. Swimming beach, archery range, hiking and cross-country ski trails on 3,000 acres. Open year-round. Located 16 miles northwest of Crivitz on Woods Lake. N10008 Paust Lane. (715) 757-3722.

Pine Acres Resort. Family resort on High Falls Flowage, which has 32 miles of wild shoreline, islands, and bays. Open year-round; amenities include paddleboats, canoe and motorized-boat rentals, snowshoe and cross-country ski trails (ski equipment available for rent). The fireplace-accented lodge serves a weekend breakfast. N10184 Parkway Road (on WI Rustic Road #32 and the Iron Snowshoe Trail). (715) 757-3894.

Popp's Resort. Anglers love this location on the wild shores of the High Falls Flowage. Trophy muskies abound, and some of Wisconsin's finest smallmouth-bass fishing is found here. Ice fishing in winter—often as early as December. Whitewater rafting is just a hop, skip, and a jump away. Lakefront cottages and vacation motel. Rene's Supper Club, known for choice steaks, offers convenient fine dining. Resort is located on the scenic Iron Snowshoe Trail. Open year-round. W11581, County X. (715) 757-3511.

MARINETTE

Best Western Riverfront Inn. Nice location in central Marinette—within walking distance of shopping, theater, and museum. Buffet breakfast included. Restaurant, indoor pool, and video games. 1821 Riverside Avenue. (715) 732-1000.

Dome Resort and Conference Center. Restaurant, indoor pool, miniature golf. Located on the shore of Green Bay and adjacent to the University of Wisconsin-Marinette Center. 751 University Drive. (715) 735-0533.

Lauerman Guest House Inn. Restored Victorian mansion filled with antiques. Inn has two whirlpools, great room with fireplace and TV, and accompanying breakfast. 1975 Riverside Avenue. (715) 732-7800.

Out to Eat
CRIVITZ

Dock Side Bar and Grill. Views aplenty from this High Falls Flowage location overlooking the Peshtigo River. This spot's claim to fame is that it serves the largest hamburger in the area. Parkway at Eagle Road. (715) 757-3244.

MARINETTE

The Brothers Three—For Hungry People. Who can resist a name like that? These folks aim to please with their homemade pizza, Italian and Mexican selections, as well as seafood and sandwiches galore. 1302 Marinette Avenue. (715) 735-9054.

Memories Restaurant. Touted as the only 1950s-style restaurant in the area, this comfy place serves homemade goodies like breads and pies and a full menu of other home-style favorites. 1378 Main Street. (715) 735-3348.

PESHTIGO

Schussler's Supper Club. If you like Old World German dishes, including schnitzel, one of the house specialties, you're going to love this supper club. American cuisine includes steak and seafood. W3529 Highway B. (715) 582-4962.

27

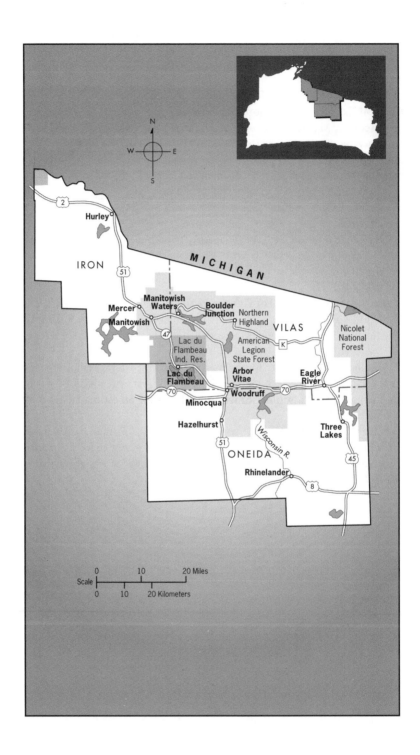

Scale
0   10   20 Miles
0   10   20 Kilometers

28

chapter 2
the Lakeland Area:
Oneida, Vilas, and Iron Counties

here are 1.1 million acres of water in Wisconsin, and a great abundance of it is located here. What else shapes the flavor of this area? Three words: lakes, fishing, and snowmobiles.

For water fanatics or those who simply love to look at lakeside views, this is your sort of place. Practically all of the natural lakes in Wisconsin have been created from glaciers, and some of the state's most beautiful lakes are found in this area.

In an area that stretches from Rhinelander to Eagle River, west to Woodruff and Minocqua, and all the way north to Hurley, the draw is the same. These old logging towns are now outposts for growing bands of tourists who just can't get enough of the area's splendid forests, wild rivers, and thousands of miles of shoreline etched along thousands of acres of open lakes. Minocqua, Woodruff, and Boulder Junction, magnets for an estimated 1.6 million visitors a year, also happen to lie in the midst of the Northern Highland— American Legion State Forest. Encompassing 220,00 acres, this is the largest of Wisconsin's state forests. The massive land area reaches from the Bearskin Trail south of Minocqua to Boulder Junction, then northwest to Manitowish Waters. The forest's 935 lakes are more reasons why this mammoth playground is such a popular destination.

If lakes are what you're after, consider the small community of Hazelhurst, south of Minocqua, where you can watch 100 miles of wilderness float past as you cruise the raw beauty of the Willow Flowage aboard a Wilderness Cruise boat.

Minocqua, sometimes called the Island City, is surrounded by 2,000 acres of water. Every conceivable water activity is at your fingertips: swimming, waterskiing, jet-skiing, canoeing, sailing, powerboating, and fishing. This region's top draw? Water exploration. From late spring to mid October, you'll feel like an early explorer as you glide along the water maneuvering your boat from one lake to another. Even if you're not a seasoned boater, rent a fishing boat, then let the motor gently purr as you guide your craft from one crystal-clear lake to the next.

For those who like to get out on the water and enjoy the scenery, this is heaven. The area boasts the largest chain of freshwater lakes in the world. Eagle River holds the supreme title with 28 sparkling jewels on which you can maneuver (it will take you all day to navigate just a few). The Manitowish Waters chain has 14 lakes of all sizes to explore, while the Cisco chain has 17, the second largest chain in the state.

There are so many lakes in this area (many are unnamed) that it seems like every visitor has a lake to call his or her own. Lakes or wetlands make up almost 40 percent of the land here, so there's no reason why you can't find your own pool of glacial beauty and enjoy it to your heart's content.

Spend only a few minutes in this area and you'll realize that this is the land of the muskie (see next page). In fact, the Boulder Junction and Minocqua areas have been in a friendly battle over the title of Muskie Capital for decades. Truth is that both areas have enough top-notch lakes where muskies hang out. But don't tell that to dyed-in-the-wool muskie fans who happen to live around Boulder Junction. They advertise the town as the Muskie Capital of the world, and they're ready to put their money where their mouth is. Just ask where the big ones are hiding and you're likely to get steered to a local guide willing to show you the ropes. Don't feel the locals are pressuring you to fish. In fact, they're just doing what comes naturally. Approximately 90 percent of the area's visitors come to the lakes intrigued with muskies and can't wait to drop a line.

When winter arrives, the entire area has a different facade, as well as the new sounds of outdoor activities. Along the multitude of cross-country ski trails and snowshoe paths, the crunch of skis and boots may be the only sounds you hear for miles.

Some of the state's most scenic cross-country ski trails are found in Oneida County. These four well-groomed trails should not be missed: Nose Lake Ski Trail, Cassian Two-Way Ski Trail, Enterprise Ski Trail, and Washburn Ski Trail. For trail maps and more information, contact Oneida County Visitor's Bureau: (800) 236-3006.

The whir of snowmobiles is another sound penetrating the winter stillness in these parts. There are so many snowmobiles, in fact, that you'll think there's one for every resident and visitor. To accommodate the influx of sleds, approximately 25,000 trails are continuously groomed by an endless number of North Woods snowmobiling clubs.

If you aren't inclined to climb on board a 400-pound sled, the other option is to watch some of the best snowmobiling events in the area. Just hang around Eagle River in January. That's where you'll find the World Championship Snowmobile Derby at the "Best Little Racetrack in the World." Can't make it in January? Then spend some time in February and you might catch another huge winter sport—dog sledding at the World Championship Oval Sled Dog Sprints.

As I made my way over glacier-carved basins and back roads and byways of this area, I was struck by the beauty of the terrain, but I was also impressed by the genuine sincerity of the people connected with this land. This is one of the most visited parts of the state, and yet the people I met here, in restau-

Muskie Madness

No doubt about it. There's a mystique surrounding the muskie (short for muskellunge), Wisconsin's official state fish. When you think of muskies, what may come to mind are sharks or even the sea monster in the film *Creature from the Black Lagoon*. Muskies, related to the northern pike, are neither monsters nor sharks, but their reputation for being difficult to catch, plus having the sharpest teeth of any freshwater fish, precedes them. Muskies are fascinating North Woods oddities due to their moody, elusive nature. Their razor-sharp canine teeth add to their monster image. And, they seem to be experts at hiding. They're seldom seen, yet many of the crystal-clear northern lakes are teeming with these missile-shaped predators.

When the number of the state's muskies began to decline in the late 1800s, the DNR began stocking the lakes (Wisconsin's northern lakes are still periodically stocked, as are its central and southern lakes). Today, muskies are found in shallow and deep water, in lakes of all sizes—wherever there is food. It's a myth that muskies are found primarily hugging the bottom of the deepest lakes. They've been seen basking in sunlight near the water's surface, but when one is seen, it's more common to find it hiding under a pier or boat. Interestingly, while many lakes have large muskie populations, muskies are not often found at the end of fishing lines. They are superb at laying low and outwitting anglers, possibly due to millions of years of evolution.

Part of the fascination with muskies is their size. Their favorite meal is fish, but they also eat large creatures like muskrat, mice, frogs, crayfish, and even ducks. When food is readily available, they grow fast—females grow considerably faster than males. A typical range for muskies is three to four feet, with 36 inches being the legal limit for bringing one in. Why are muskies so big today? Because many are thrown back when they're in the three-foot range. Years ago, these muskies would have been dead muskies.

Many world record muskies have been caught in Wisconsin's lakes region. All you have to do is look around Minocqua or Boulder Junction, and you're bound to see the latest muskie catches posted in the local newspaper or at inns and restaurants. One example of a huge muskie is the one caught in Lake Superior around the turn of the century. This giant was purported to weigh in at 102 pounds, but the report is undocumented.

Should you worry about muskies biting you? It's highly unlikely that a swimmer or water-skier will be attacked by one. It's more likely that a muskie will swim away from movement in the water. Nevertheless, it pays to err on the side of safety. One muskie story got a lot of press in the summer of 1998. A man dangling his foot over the side of a canoe in Twin Valley Lake in Governor Dodge State Park, west of Madison, found out that muskie teeth are sharp and can cause a lot of pain. Since this fish caught the man, and not the other way around, the story set off speculation that man-eating muskies were running rampant. While this story is true—the man required several stitches—it's also fair to say that muskies unmistakably prefer fish and small game to humans.

When is the best time of year to land a muskie? It depends on whom you're talking to, but generally the best fishing runs from May to November, with October being the favorite month of serious anglers. Muskies like cold water, so early spring or late fall offer the best times for landing one.

31

rants, lodges, inns, and other busy places, seemed to thrive on the excitement of the sheer number of people they encountered. Rather than being jaded by the onslaught of visitors and their repetitive questions about finding North Woods treasures like the elusive muskie and the best pizza, locals seemed fueled with a steady stream of enthusiasm.

There are a few local folks whose friendly and helpful manner made a difference to this North Woods visitor. When I locked myself out of my car in the driveway of the Cranberry Hill Inn in Rhinelander, the inn's owner, Karen Minassi, accepted the dilemma as a personal challenge. Have you ever tried to find a locksmith on a Sunday afternoon? It's not easy, but Karen found one. She put her own plans of taking her kids to a movie on hold and furiously worked the Yellow Pages. She found a locksmith who not only was willing to come over from a neighboring town who but also accepted my American Automobile Association card without charging an arm and a leg. In the meantime, Karen offered up a plate of just-baked cookies and strong coffee, just the way I like it.

Then there was Dan, a local resident about to enter his first year at George Washington University. Dan was working to pay his college tuition by being a summer server at Paul Bunyan's Cook Shanty between Minocqua and Woodruff. He had been working at this same restaurant since eighth grade. He said he rode his bike to work, sometimes starting out at 6:00 A.M., to get ready for the daily "ranch hands" breakfast. What I liked most about this standout waiter was the fact that he obviously enjoyed his job and the restaurant's nonstop stampede of people. His enthusiasm was contagious. He encouraged me to try everything—he brought dishes that he thought I'd like (all under the one-price meal plan) because, heaven forbid, I might miss a good thing. In more than one taste test, he was right.

Then too, Dick and Carol Malmgren, owners of White Birch Village in Boulder Junction, found, on a moment's notice, a place for my family to stay in one of their spectacular vacation homes. Although a last-minute cancellation by another guest was the reason for my good fortune, the Malmgrens went into high gear to make our stay relaxing and memorable.

Sure, the area has a large number of visitors each year. And for some, the thought of urbanlike traffic on Highway 51, the main north-south route through the area, is daunting. Yet, after you've explored the lakes region for a while, you'll find it's easy to get around and discover your own piece of paradise. Then all you have to decide is what you want to do. Choices for year-round recreation and relaxation are endless.

Rhinelander

Rhinelander, a former logging and lumber boomtown located on appropriately named Boom Lake (one of 1,100 lakes in Oneida County), is a year-round playground for anglers, campers, nature lovers, and snowmobilers.

The county also has more than 50 trout streams. This territory is the gateway to the vast Northern Highlands—American Legion State Forest and to the profusion of lakes around Rhinelander and to the north. Here's a lake fact to stagger the imagination: If you're standing in downtown Rhinelander, you're within a 10-mile circle encompassing 235 lakes.

COURTESY OF JOHN CZARNEZKI

One of the Rhinelander area's pristine lakes in autumn.

Don't leave Rhinelander without getting a look at the town's early logging days. You'll find plenty of signs pointing to the Logging Museum, where lumberjack life is highlighted. Countless sawmills were once part of the landscape around here. The area's numerous lakes and rivers served as main arteries for moving mountains of northern timber to the mills. Once railroads established a Rhinelander connection, area businesses began diversifying their products, the most important of which was paper. Papermaking became such a successful venture that today it remains one of the town's prime industries.

Besides Rhinelander's legendary logging days, "hodags" are another reason you won't forget this place. These horrible looking creatures straight out of North Woods folklore are found at only two places in the world. What a coincidence that they're both in Rhinelander—at the Logging Museum and the Chamber of Commerce. Some visitors are sure that there are real hodags lurking in Rhinelander's woods. I've been in restaurants and gas stations where I've heard people ask where they can see them. One of the answers is that they are on sweatshirts and souvenirs all over town.

The hodag myth started in 1896 when Rhinelander pioneer Gene Shepard told his lumberjack friends that he had seen a hairy monster, seven-feet long and thirty-inches high, with large white horns on its back. The beast had sharp tusks surrounding its jaw and short muscular legs stocked with razor-sharp extensions.

Shepard's group was so enthralled with the tale that they took to the woods to capture the beast. Shepard and his pals supposedly captured it in a cave by extending the end of a long bamboo pole with a chloroform-soaked cloth into the hodag's mouth. The excited lumberjacks then dragged it back to Shepard's house. It doesn't seem to matter to those eager to investigate the hodag yarn that the beast supposedly escaped and that later Shepard admitted he had made up the story. He had elaborately created the fake animal by using a mixture of metal and animal skins. The pit, though, where the hodag was supposedly confined is still part of Shepard's lawn.

By the way, if you travel to Rhinelander with a white bulldog, consider yourself forewarned. White bulldogs are considered to be a hodag delicacy.

For more information contact the Rhinelander Area Chamber of Commerce: (715) 365-7464 or (800) 236-4FUN.

Sights and Attractions

Logging Museum. Several buildings, including an old logging camp dining room, the restored Soo Line Depot, a one-room schoolhouse, and Civilian Conservation Corps Museum. Enough logging memorabilia and local history to easily fill up an hour or two. Located in Pioneer Park, downtown Rhinelander, one block off Business 8. Open daily, mid-May to mid-September, 10:00 A.M. to 5:00 P.M. No admission. (715) 369-5004 or (715) 362-2193.

Oneida County Courthouse. The Tiffany glass in the building's dramatic dome is a special attraction at night. Tour the inside of the courthouse to gain insight into area history. In particular, the beautiful murals depicting pioneer life make you realize that these area artists had a special knack for artistic storytelling.

Events

Colorama Fly-In. Held in September, this event is sponsored by the Northwoods Aviation Association to promote North Woods aviation. You can catch a ride on an airplane, helicopter, sailplane, or biplane. The Fly-In is held at the Rhinelander/Oneida County Airport. Admission and parking are free.

The Great Hodag Duck Chase Festival. This three-day festival in early August features a rubber-duck race on the Wisconsin River, canoe and bike races, "waddle runs," and, of course, food booths, live music, and plenty of arts and crafts. (Never let it be said that North Woods marketing gurus aren't wizards when it comes to devising clever gimmicks to attract crowds.)

The Hodag Water Ski Shows. College kids home for the summer, and others, perform a variety of acts, all on the water, under the lights. Mid-June through late August every Thursday and Sunday evening. The fun starts at 7:30 on Boom Lake at Hodag Park. Take Stevens Street north through Rhinelander, then follow the signs to the park.

Lodging

Cranberry Hill Inn Bed and Breakfast. This elaborate mansion was built in 1890 for former lumber baron E. O. Brown, who wanted a fitting residence for his wife, Clara. The sumptuous home has been beautifully restored and updated. Brown, a Rhinelander pioneer, was the force behind the Brown Lumber Company, the Rhinelander Paper Mill, the first refrigeration company in Rhinelander, and the Merchants State Bank. Owner Karen Minassi has added brilliant touches of period decor and antiques. This unforgettable landmark features a dining room done in navy and white, a gargantuan library, and a bedroom so huge it easily holds four beds. 209 E. Frederick Street. (715) 369-3504.

Fease's Shady Rest Lodge. Since 1955 the main attraction here is the pristine setting and the lakefront views of picturesque Manson Lake. Located on Breezy Point Peninsula, this spot is perfect for a family getaway. Lodging choices include rooms in the main lodge or furnished cabins. At your fingertips are a large number of activities, including waterskiing (lessons available too), renting a pontoon boat, and playing shuffleboard. At this North Woods lodge you'll find a recreation building and hearty food (served when you want it) as part of your package. 8440 Shady Rest Road. (715) 282-5231 or (800) 477-3229.

Holiday Acres. Offers the epitome of a family resort package. Rooms are available in the main lodge, but most visitors want their own cottage, which comes with a boat. The list of activities is dazzling. The resort's amenities include the Hodag Snow Trail (snowmobiling), which passes through the property, 11 miles of cross-country ski trails (good bike trails in warmer sea-

By Air

For those flying into the area, the Rhinelander/Oneida County Airport, (715) 365-3416, is served by Northwest Airlink, Skyway Airlines, and United Express. All major car rental agencies are represented at the airport. For leisurely meals or eating on the run, the Skyview Cafe serves breakfast, lunch, and fast food seven days a week. Tired of flying commercial? Then why not take flying lessons for an alternative adventure? Rhinelander Flying Service can get you off the ground. (715) 365-3456.

35

sons), 3 tennis courts, and an indoor pool. The Three Coins dining room is not to be missed. A North Woods institution. U.S. 8, approximately four miles east of Rhinelander. (715) 369-1500 or (800) 261-1500.

Holiday Inn. Located on the Northwoods Passage Snowmobile Trail, the inn features an indoor swimming pool, Jacuzzi, sauna, and exercise room. The Alpine Dining Room features a nice selection of continental favorites. 668 W. Kemp. (715) 369-3600 or (800) HOLIDAY.

Out to Eat

Al Gen Dinner Club. The Al Gen (you can't miss it, with the big "The Al Gen" sign on the log building's roof), owned by Rob and Amy Swearingen, sports a rustic supper club atmosphere complete with game room, kids' menu, and a plethora of house specialties. Regulars come back for the Black Angus prime rib, broasted chicken, roast duck, tenderloin Oscar, and deep-fried baby walleye. One half mile east of Sunrise Plaza, just off U.S. 8. Open at 4:30 P.M., Tuesdays through Sundays. Like many North Woods supper clubs, they're closed on Mondays. (715) 362-2230.

JME Café and General Store. Take a step back to yesteryear and stop at this authentic roadhouse café in Gleason, between Rhinelander and Merrill. The town, which advertises itself as a trout fishing mecca, has fallen into oblivion, now that most motorists take Highway 51 into the lakes area, but the cafe and the old-time general store and grocery are worth a side trip.

In the tiny dining area I sat next to a row of old photos depicting area landmarks. One black-and-white oldie featured lumberjacks chopping down "the last big tree" in the area in 1937. The huge elm is now showcased on the courthouse square in Merrill. I enjoyed a delicious chicken sandwich on whole-wheat bread for a grand total of $1.50. Besides sandwiches and daily specials, breakfast is also served. The cafe is open daily from 5:00 A.M. to 8:00 P.M. The general store has a variety of usual and unusual items, including pasta, spices, and dried food in bulk. On WI 17. (715) 873-4043.

Rhinelander Cafe and Pub. Possibly the most popular eating place in town. It's also the oldest—it's been going strong since 1911. The cavernous ballroom-sized pub serves everything from sandwiches to steaks. Breakfast, lunch, and dinners are served. Open daily, 7:00 A.M. to 10:30 P.M. 33 N. Brown Street (you can also enter via the second entrance on Courtney Street). (715) 362-2918.

Shopping

Finishing Touches. This huge red-brick, 100-year-old-plus Victorian mansion contains a gift shop, art gallery, and studio for artists' supplies. If you have the time, take classes in watercolor or rosemaling (Scandinavian floral painting) from the resident artist. The story goes that there was once a tunnel in the basement so that a long-ago former owner could get to his brewery across the street. Open Monday through Saturday. 919 Arbitus

Street (near the hospital). (715) 369-3544.

Three Lakes

If you're headed to the North Woods via U.S. 45, southeast of Eagle River, you'll come to Three Lakes, a no-nonsense sort of retreat where serious sports enthusiasts like to congregate. Three Lakes is a sports and recreation center because it's on the cusp of the Eagle River District of the Nicolet National Forest. If you haven't gotten yourself oriented before you arrive, stop at the Three Lakes Information Bureau, located in a small log building on U.S. 45, just south of town. The cozy cabin is well stocked with information and enjoys a nice location, across from historic St. Theresa Church, with its towering steeple, ruby red doors, and magnificent stained-glass windows. Visitors to Three Lakes on Sunday mornings can't miss hearing the church's splendid carillon bells.

The Three Lakes and Eagle River area attracts visitors because of its proximity to the eastern side of the Nicolet National Forest. Swimming, boating, canoeing, hiking, and biking are all part of the Nicolet experience. Of the forest's more than 600,000 acres, over 33,000 are wilderness areas for backpacking. Over 520 miles are designated cross-country ski trails or interpretive and snowmobile trails. For information about the Eagle River district of the forest (there are three other districts, Laona, Florence, and Lakewood), **contact the Eagle River Ranger Station, 434 Wall Street, Eagle River, (715) 479-2827.** It's more likely to have a bigger selection of maps and information than the forest's headquarters in Rhinelander.

Sights and Attractions

Concerts in the Park. At the new gazebo (built in 1996) in Cy Williams Park. Free performances range from Dixieland bands, to vocalists, to string ensembles. From early July to late August, 7:00 P.M. Bring your own chair. The alternate rain location is at St. Theresa's Church on U.S. 45.

Hiking and Biking Trails. Four are known for their majestic beauty: (1) Giant Pine Trail, which is particularly well designed for hikers (take WI 32 southeast of Three Lakes, then watch for the sign to the trail); (2) Luna-White Deer Hiking Trail, a 4.5-mile trail that begins at the campground of White Deer Beach, then makes its way around Luna and White Deer Lakes; (3) Sam Campbell Memorial Forest and Hiking Trail Complex, northeast of Three Lakes, off Military Road (Forest Road 2178) on the old Military Trail (Forest Road 2207); (4) Spectacle Lake and Kentuck Lake Trail, a 2.5-mile trail connecting two campgrounds on the shores of these lakes. Maps and information are available at the Three Lakes Information Bureau, (800) 972-6103 or (715) 546-3344, or at the U.S. Forest Service in Eagle River, (715) 479-2827.

Three Lakes Historical Museum. Don't drive by because the spot doesn't grab your attention. The somewhat nondescript buildings (one of the buildings is a recreated Civilian Conservation Corps bunkhouse) are much more interesting inside. You'll see all sorts of memorabilia of Sam Campbell, a familiar name in these parts, who is often referred to as the "Philosopher of the Forest." The displays of pioneer logging and hand tools, clothing, and musical instruments are interesting; also featured are a flower garden comprising pioneer plant varieties and rarely seen genealogy files. Free admission. Open daily, Memorial Day through September, 10 A.M to 4 P.M. 1798 Huron Street. (715) 546-2295.

Three Lakes Winery. For over 25 years as a fixture in the community, the winery is the dream come true of John and Maureen McCain, who moved their family from California to Three Lakes so they could try their skills at making cranberry wines. The move paid off—the winery now produces more than a dozen wines, including cranberry, blackberry, strawberry-rhubarb, Granny Smith apple, and red raspberry. Gourmet foods and gifts are also available. Open seven days a week. Free wine tasting and winery tours. Downtown Three Lakes at the corner of U.S. 45, WI 32, and County A. (800) 944-5434 or (715) 546-3080.

Out to Eat

Black Forest Pub and Grille. You name it, it's probably on this eclectic menu—everything from nachos and quesadillas, to Chicago-style Italian beef sandwiches, blackened pork chops, and New York strip steaks. Also enjoy the bountiful cod and walleye fish fry every Friday night. Fun atmosphere. Downtown Three Lakes on Superior Street. (715) 546-3400.

J. J.'s Dog House. If the smell of pines and campfires make you long for old-fashioned hot dogs, you've come to the right place. Customers gather here for Chicago-style Vienna red-hots, brats, and fully stuffed sandwiches and subs. The restaurant also whips up a mean old-fashioned root beer float. 1792 Superior Street. (715) 546-2119.

John Henry's Supper Club. Steaks, seafood, prime rib, chicken, and all the trimmings. A house specialty are the succulent, slow-cooked barbecued ribs. Nice setting on Spirit Lake. One mile east of Three Lakes on 1426 WI 32. Open Tuesday through Sunday from 4:30 P.M. (715) 546-2929.

Shopping

The Hodge Podge Lodge. In this small northern town you might not expect to find a large gathering of artistic treasures, but here it is. The Hodge Podge (rightly named) is a mix of 29 shops filled with art and collectibles from over 225 artists. Everything from toys, quilts, paintings, clothing, and jewelry are waiting to go home with you. 1760 Superior Street. (715) 546-8141.

Eagle River

Thinking about sitting back and soaking up some North Woods water, woods, and wildlife? Then join the pack of fans who converge on the Eagle

River District of the Nicolet National Forest and the area's chain of 28 lakes—the world's largest freshwater chain.

There's so much going on, it's hard to know where to start. The calendar is packed, particularly from late spring to early fall, with arts and crafts festivals, fishing and cranberry festivals, world-class snowmobile races in January, and dogsled races in February. And you'll find an abundance of historical museums, antique and specialty shops, good restaurants, and memorable lodges.

Those two trappers, Bethuel Draper and "Dutch Pete" Cramer, who in 1853 supposedly named the place because they were enthralled with the abundance of eagle pairs on Eagle River, would be amazed at today's development. The town, with a predominance of restaurants, lodges, and entertainment spots, is a far cry from what it used to be in 1890, when there were 22 taverns and 1 church.

Once Eagle River's trapping industry slowed down, logging came on strong, but by 1910, the area's great white pines were nearly all logged out. It's probably no surprise that tourism took over after World War I, when more people owned automobiles and could get to this North Woods destination. Yet curious visitors found the area well before that, as early as 1877. Even after World War I, when many were traveling by automobile, the majority of visitors still arrived via the Chicago and North Western Railroad. In Eagle River these folks were met at the depot by shuttle boats, then taken over the lakes to their destination. Visitors couldn't get enough of the chain of 28 lakes—which incidentally, because few portages existed after linking up with the Wisconsin River, made it possible to paddle to your heart's content from Eagle River all the way to New Orleans.

By 1925 there were 29 resorts in Vilas County. Some of the well-known 1920s lodges include the Chanticleer Inn, the Hiawatha Lodge, and Big Bass Resort. Today there are hundreds of places to stay in the area. **If you don't have a spot in mind before you arrive, stop at the Eagle River Area Chamber of Commerce Visitors Center in the old Chicago and North Western Railroad Depot, built in the 1920s, on Railroad Street. (800) 359-6315.**

Our family had come to get away from it all. But we didn't want to be too far out in the woods. We settled on the **Pine-Aire Resort and Campground** because we heard it was geared to family members of all ages. I called early because I wanted one of the six waterfront cottages. A nice fully equipped, two-bedroom cottage, with fireplace, was ours for a week.

We don't live close to a lake at home so this spot was an exciting change. The kids had a hard time breaking away from watching the boating and fishing from the small dock only yards from our back door. Attached to the pier was a rowboat awaiting our arrival. A short distance down the water's edge, a larger pier served as the rental headquarters for outboard motors. The kids could hardly wait to row to that dock and have a motor put on.

The next morning they got their wish. Once we were powered, we began touring the lake, navigating through a narrow passage into a second lake, then a third. All the while we enjoyed the magnificent scenery of white aspen and birch reflecting off crisp blue water. Soon we found out we could visit several businesses by boat. Plenty of restaurants and shops expect you to pull up, tie a line, and come in.

When we returned to our cottage, the adjacent campground was ablaze with campfires. People were trading fishing and boating stories. Teenagers were preparing for a beach party with a DJ, and the full-time recreational director passed through trying to drum up interest in the "professional stage entertainment" at one of the lodge buildings.

The next morning the kids were anxious to get back on the water and navigate a few more lakes. This lake-conquest thing was what we had come for, after all.

Nearly one-third of the country's residents live within 500 miles of Wisconsin. If you polled them for a definition of the North Woods, they would probably describe Eagle River or a fictional place that really was Eagle River in disguise. Why here, you wonder? The magic is in the mix, so they say. Here you have the beauty of the wilderness and endless lakes, along with pancake palaces, moccasin outlets, and lots of restaurants, lodges, motels, and entertainment spots, all coexisting nicely. The combination isn't for everyone, to be sure, but a lot of people sure like the diversity.

Sights and Attractions

Carl's Wood Art Museum. Carl Schels Sr. immigrated from Bavaria decades ago and eventually settled in the North Woods, making a name for himself by carving mammoth replicas of wildlife. His wood art, created by chain saws, includes a 14-foot, 5,000-pound grizzly bear. The awe-inspiring museum (and gift shop) is open Memorial Day weekend through mid-October. 1230 Sundstein Road, two blocks west of McDonald's. (715) 479-1883.

Eagle River Golf Course. A picturesque 18-hole course. You can reserve tee times up to 14 days in advance. 527 McKinley Blvd. Take U.S. 45 north of the Eagle River bridge, then turn right on McKinley Blvd. (800) 280-1477.

Eagle River Historical Museum. This new museum opened in 1998 on the Trees for Tomorrow site, the Midwest's oldest natural resource teaching facility. Follow a half-mile demonstration trail at Trees for Tomorrow, an innovative spot listed on the National Register of Historic Places. You'll see a variety of trees at many levels of growth. There are 150-year-old pines and 10-year-old aspens, all within a small space. Most of the buildings were built by the Civilian Conservation Corps in the 1930s. Trees for Tomorrow is still used by students and teachers from a three-state area as a North Woods learning lab. 519 Sheridan Street East. For more information, contact the Eagle River Information Bureau, (715) 479-2396.

Lake Forest Golf Course. A nine-hole course with lots of history going back to 1917, when a few wealthy golf aficionados opened their own private club. Dwight Eisenhower was a regular player in the 1950s. Golf course, restaurant, and fitness center are open to the public. 3801 Eagle River Road. Take WI 70 four and a half miles east of Eagle River. (800) 830-0471.

Northwoods Children's Museum. This interactive spot features an ice castle, fishing pond, shadow room, grocery store, medical center, and even a bubble station-clever ideas conceived to enrich children's (and parent's) lives. The idea for the museum started in 1993 and became a reality in 1998. A good hands-on spot. One example: watch for forest fires at the museum's fire station. 346 W. Division Street. (715) 479-4623.

Events

Cranberry Fest. The event runs over five days during the first week of October, with cranberry celebrations extraordinaire. Sample cranberry fritters, ice cream, meatballs, soups, and more. Also featured are arts and crafts, antiques, entertainment, a walk, and fun run. If you like festivals, this is one of Wisconsin's most intriguing. At the Vilas County Fairgrounds. Shuttles take you from downtown Eagle River. For more information call the Eagle River Area Chamber of Commerce and Visitors Center, (800) 359-6315.

Great Annual Bicycle Adventure along the Wisconsin River (GRABA AWR). Over 1,300 participants annually look forward to this late-June bike adventure. They begin at Eagle River, then make their way over 450 miles to Prairie du Chien in southeastern Wisconsin, where the Wisconsin and Mississippi Rivers converge.

Klondike Days. If you've never seen a dogsled race, this is the place to get initiated. Promoted as "the fastest sled dog racing in the world," this mid-February, two-day event takes place at the same track as the snowmobile derby. For more information call (800) 359-6315.

Valvoline World Championship Snowmobile Derby. Tourists weren't flocking to Eagle River in the middle of the winter some 35 years ago. But thanks to the efforts of 10 area businessmen who saw a future in that new contraption, the snowmobile, the area now flourishes when it's cold. For five days in mid-January, snowmobiles reign supreme at the local snowmobile track, with a natural "bowl" configuration; it's been called "the best little racetrack in the world." U.S. 45 North. For more information contact the derby office, (715) 479-4424.

Lodging

The Braywood. Built by Billy Bray and Frances Woods in 1949, well-known dancers who often performed with Lawrence Welk, Guy Lombardo, and other big names. The lodge's claim to fame is that it was the first Northern Wisconsin lakeshore resort built with private baths. The resort's location on Catfish Lake features boat rentals, a children's play area, golf and fishing packages, and many other amenities. The restaurant (regulars return for the famous Brayburger and other burgers with an attitude) and cocktail lounge are popular unwinding spots. Motel units, suites, or cottage are available. Open year-round. U.S. 45 on Catfish Lake Road, one and a half miles south of Eagle River. (715) 479-6494.

Chanticleer Inn. One of the area's famous resorts going back to 1922. Family owned, the resort's accommodations range from motel rooms to villas on 40 acres of wooded property on Voyageur Lake. Outdoor beer garden, two sandy beaches, two tennis courts and more. Well-known dining room offers outstanding fare such as swordfish and tasty chicken dishes. 1458 E. Dollar Road. (715) 479-4486 or (800) 752-9193.

Eagle Waters Resort. This historic property traces its beginning to 1850, when the first North Woods trading post was located here. Later on, county residents cast 700 votes here for Abraham Lincoln in his bid for the presidency. The settlement was also used as a bank and post office before becoming the Eagle Waters Resort in 1883. Over the years many weddings have been celebrated on the property, and the tradition has been to plant a tree in honor of each married couple. Consequently, the property is the site of many stands of old trees. Cabins, condos, and motel rooms are available. Enjoy casual dining (buckets of chicken to go), popular Friday-night fish fries, and Sunday brunch. 3958 Eagle Waters Road. (800) 8-WATERS.

Gypsy Villa. If you're looking for privacy and a sense of adventure, this is it. You can choose to stay on 100-acre Cranberry Island, with 14 yellow and brown cottages dotting the landscape. Other cottages, villas, and condominiums are located on the mainland. Comfortable units feature screened porches, TVs, fireplaces, a fishing boat or pontoon boat, and a private pier. What more could you want? What about organized sing-alongs and treasure hunts? That's what returning guests often remember the most. Open year-round. 950 Circle Drive. (715) 479-8644.

The Inn at Pinewood. This is a bed and breakfast with the feeling of quiet elegance a la a North Woods lodge. On a beautiful setting on Carpenter Lake, this romantic hideaway has charming guest rooms, some with whirlpool baths and fireplaces. This 21-room inn provides delicious breakfasts, including homemade muffins and breads, with your stay. Open year-round. 1820 Silver Forest Lane. (715) 477-2377.

Pine-Aire Resort and Campground. If only the walls could talk. Generations of visitors have fond memories of their stays here since the 1920s, when the property was a children's camp. It seems like a mini-North Woods town in itself, with campgrounds, cottages (one deluxe cottage has a fireplace, air conditioning, and a whirlpool), entertainment, and family campfire activities. The Logging Camp Kitchen restaurant can turn into a place where vaudeville meets the North Woods when campers and resort guests show up in costume for a theme party. Serves bountiful and hearty breakfasts, Imaginative dinners include veal chardonnay with mushrooms and pork filet; also known for good Mexican fare. Two miles north of Eagle River on U.S. 45, on Chain of Lakes Road, on the Eagle Chain of Lakes. Open year-round. (715) 479-9208 or (800) 597-6777.

Out to Eat

Alexander's Pizza. You have to believe the pizza is good if participants in a University of Wisconsin Business School survey say so. Not long ago, its Small Business Institute conducted a survey of 11 Eagle River pizza parlors to determine who had the area's best pie at the best price. Alexander's came out on top, and they won't let you forget it. Pizzas are baked on a stone hearth, like they do in old Italy. Downtown Eagle River. (715) 479-7363.

Baertschy's Pine Gables. Offers traditional German dishes, such as rouladen and schweinebraten, plus a mix of northern Italian cuisine, seafood (including grilled swordfish steaks), beef filet, and tenderloin from the grill. The menu is diverse (if you already hadn't guessed) and goes on to include nightly specials like veal scallopini stuffed with Montrachet goat cheese. Located in a 1938 pine building on WI 70 West. Open Tuesday through Sunday starting at 4:30 P.M. (715) 479-7689.

Captain Nemo's. Charcoal-broiled steaks and fresh trout are house specialties. While you wait, gaze at eight tanks of aquatic captives that include muskie and walleye. Supper club atmosphere with a Cajun touch. Open daily (closed Monday) beginning at 5 P.M. 3310 WI 70 East. (715) 479 2250.

The Copper Kettle. Unassuming place with a big reputation. It originally opened in nearby Three Lakes, then moved to downtown Eagle River. In 1977 the owners created the Pancake Hall of Fame after a 15 year old consumed 10 mammoth pancakes. The title, as you can see when you get here, has been surpassed many times since. Besides pancakes, the restaurant also serves other family fare such as soups and sandwiches. Open daily 7 A.M. to 10 P.M. 207 E. Wall Street. (715) 479-4049.

Shopping

Eagle River is brimming with interesting shops. Here are just a few samples.

Bonson's Fine Foods. This is a deli, bakery, meat, floral, gift, and produce shop all rolled into one. For over 50 years Bonson's has been baking a variety of goodies, but their famous Danish kringle is probably the most famous. The ring-shaped pastry comes in 10 flavors, including apple, raspberry, and blueberry. Up north during a birthday or anniversary? Head to Bonson's floral department—their "Stuffin" system stuffs your gift inside a balloon. Open seven days a week. U.S. 45 North, in the Vilas Village Mall. (715) 479-4416

Chain of Lakes Cyclery. The circa 1883 building has long been a fixture in downtown Eagle River. It first housed a hardware store, then a meat market and grocery store. Bradner's Market operated here for over 60 years, until 1991. In 1997 the cyclery set up shop offering bike and ski sales and rentals. 107 N. Railroad Street. (715) 479-3920.

Moccasin Shop and Treasure Chest. What's a visit to the North Woods without making at least one moccasin run? (The favored Minnetonka brand is actually made in Minnesota.) This downtown landmark, filled with Eagle River souvenirs, claims to have the largest moccasin selection in the area. 101 E. Wall Street. (715) 479-7100.

Hazelhurst, Minocqua, Woodruff, Arbor Vitae

Between Memorial Day and Labor Day, expect crowds of tourists—all with seemingly one thing in mind—to get on or near one of the area's 3,200 lakes. No wonder this is called the Lakeland area.

During the peak of the summer tourist season, you know you're getting close to where the action is when you get to Hazelhurst, on U.S. 51, the main north-south artery, 10 miles south of Minocqua. This is where traffic begins to slow and an endless parade of motorists is characterized by the passionate pursuit of recreation. Take a look at the majority of cars and vans coming into the area. You'll see that they have one thing in common-most are hauling boats, trailers, and jet skis.

Many of these hordes of travelers are staying in the area. But don't let that frighten you from claiming your own back-to-nature piece of paradise. The area is well prepared for the annual onslaught. You'll find a vast array of lodges, inns, motels, cabins, and resorts to choose from. Other visitors find the Minocqua area to be a good jumping-off point to other woods and water destinations in the North Woods. That means you'll find plenty of places providing provisions, everything from clothing and sporting-goods stores to marinas with boats for rent.

Fishing is the number-one reason many visitors hang out here. You're reminded of that fact, that fishing in these well-stocked lakes is great, over and over again. If you don't fish, chances are you'll be tempted to take it up before you leave. Local hype makes you feel that all you have to do is put some time and energy into the sport, and you too can catch that big one. It's akin to walking around a carnival midway and seeing people carrying giant teddy bears—prize trophies from throwing baseballs at milk bottles. Seeing is believing, so they say. It makes you feel you can do it too.

The Minocqua area is rather like that. Forty-inch-plus stuffed muskies make their appearance above numerous restaurant doorways and in local haunts. Even if you don't fish, you can understand the excitement that overtakes fishing fanatics when you see so many enormous fish taken from the same lake you're gazing at. (Fishing aficionados don't seem to care that, on average, it takes 100 fishing hours to catch a 33-inch muskie.)

Fishing mania is such a natural occurrence around here, it's part of the language of the highway. Go north on U.S. 51 between Minocqua and Woodruff, and you'll see a sign among the fast-food establishments, "Leeches $9.50 a pound." Or stop at one of the gas stations in Minocqua, and you're likely to see the counters plastered with photos of people who have caught huge muskies in the surrounding lakes.

If fishing is your passion, you're bound to have fun in this legendary fishing mecca. The area around Hazelhurst, Minocqua, Woodruff, and Arbor Vitae is known for having one of the largest freshwater groups of lakes in the world.

Equally remarkable are the countless numbers of streams, brooks, and ponds that are home to sport fish and panfish. Plus, this area is the headwaters for the Wisconsin River and the Chippewa-Flambeau River system, the two largest river basins in the state.

For inside fishing information, hire a fishing guide. The area Chamber of Commerce can help you find one from the numerous operators in the area. These are some of the more well-known guides and outfitters.

Darrell Mittlesteadt's Fishing Guidelines Guide Service. Specializes in walleye, muskie, and bass. Woodruff. (715) 356-7387.

Jeff Winters Guide Service. All ages welcome—that means kids too. Lunches, full- or half-day guide services. Woodruff. (715) 385-9313.

Lake Minocqua Guide Service. They fish for all varieties on full- or half-day outings. Minocqua. (715) 356-3288.

Mundt's. One-stop fishing spot. If you're going fishing, they've got it. Bait, tackle, all the provisions. Arbor Vitae (715) 358-2147.

Rollie and Helen's Muskie Shop. Purported to be the "world's largest muskie shop." Offers guide service, tackle, and bait, and specializes in (what else?) fishing for muskies. Minocqua. (715) 356-6011.

Strictly Walleye/Muskie Headquarters. No guessing what they specialize in. These people are serious threats to any fish on the lakes. Minocqua. (715) 356-9229.

Swimmer's Itch

In the North Woods, if you plan to frolic in many of its lakes, be prepared for a condition called swimmer's itch. What is it? It's caused by microscopic parasites that get inside the skin and cause serious itching. Once these tiny creatures burrow their way inside the body, they die, but the itching can go on for several days.

Symptoms include swelling and a red spot on the skin where the parasites have penetrated and begin to grow, a condition that becomes worse if the area is scratched. In severe cases the person may have a fever and feel nauseous. In these cases a physician should be contacted. Otherwise, the itch usually disappears within a few days.

How can you avoid getting swimmer's itch?
• Don't swim in shallow water near the shore. Parasites tend to be more prevalent near the water's edge. Children are more susceptible to getting swimmer's itch because they are more apt to play near shore.
• Resist temptation and don't feed ducks and birds near the shore. They are often carriers of the parasite.
• Avoid swimming in areas with snails—they too are hosts for the parasite.
• Dry yourself off immediately after swimming.
• Don't swim immediately after an onshore wind.

Making your way in downtown Minocqua is easy. If you're here for a short time and like walking to sites and shops, a good choice for lodging is the New Concord Inn, from which you can walk anywhere in the downtown area. You'll hear locals make reference to a location by saying, "It's above or below the bridge." Coming into Minocqua from the south on U.S. 51, you'll see that the road runs in two directions, splits at the bridge before you get to the downtown, then becomes a one-way artery looping around the town. Finding a parking lot is easy in the downtown area—lots are simply marked A, B, or C.

Long a favorite place for summering Chicagoans, Minocqua is still a favorite retreat with folks from the Windy City as well as other urban dwellers. Maybe that's because here you can have your cake and eat it too. Visitors can indulge themselves in that get-away-from-it-all feeling, particularly at lakeside hideaways. But even out in the woods, you're never far from good restaurants, upscale shopping malls, and a kaleidoscope of activities for kids.

Minocqua's interest in keeping visitors entertained translates to a small-town atmosphere alive with a cosmopolitan flavor. To get your bearings, stop at the new rustic North Woods Chamber of Commerce building on U.S. 51, south of Minocqua, next to the Red Steer Supper Club. **Minocqua-Arbor Vitae-Woodruff Area Chamber of Commerce. (715) 356-5266 or (800) 44-NORTH.** A huge assortment of free information is yours for the asking.

Just a mile or so north on U.S. 51, Woodruff, Minocqua's unpretentious sister city, has a less snazzy facade. As a destination, Woodruff draws hikers, campers and cross-country skiers. If you are in the area for these activities, stop at the main ranger station at Trout Lake, about seven miles north of U.S. 51 on County M, for trail and camping information. (715) 385-2727.

Speaking of Trout Lake, one of the most nostalgic spots in Wisconsin's North Woods is located here. This is **Coon's Franklin Lodge**, a 250-acre resort run by the fourth generation of the Coon family. Sit on the front porch of the main log lodge or on a comfortable chair in front of your own log cabin (the resort has 27) and picture how it might have been 100 years ago when the local steamer shuttled guests back and forth across the lake. Wilderness with style, that's Coon's special touch. An old-fashioned dinner bell announces meals three times a day, summoning guests into the old octagonal dining room. Delicious breads, cakes, and pies are all part of the atmosphere. Open June to September. 3450 Highway U.S. 51 North. (715) 385-2700.

The tiny town of Arbor Vitae also draws its share of tourists seeking a change of pace in the North Woods. Arbor Vitae means "tree of life," a description coined by early French explorers in recognition of the area's abundance of white cedar.

Sights and Attractions

Bearskin State Trail. This crushed red granite trail runs from Minocqua to Harshaw. In 1973 the Department of Natural Resources bought and developed abandoned railroad grades along Bearskin Creek. It's a great path to see the diversity of the North Woods, and to hike, bike, or snowmobile. The 18-mile trail traverses a wide variety of terrain, from bluffs and cliffs to flat leaf-covered segments. Not all of the trail is surfaced. Open year-round. Bikers (16 and older) pay a daily fee of $3 or a $10 seasonal fee. No fee for snowmobiling. For more information call the area Chamber of Commerce, (800) 446-6784.

Dr. Kate Museum. Woodruff. Sound unusual? It sure is, but isn't that what you came to the North Woods for, to find out what makes this area tick? This small brown log museum, affiliated with the State Historical Society, at the intersection of Second Avenue and U.S. 51, fills the bill. Changing exhibits celebrate the life of Dr. Kate Pelham, a country doctor, also known as "The Angel on Snowshoes." Discover how this humble North Woods physician inspired schoolchildren to collect a million pennies (the penny campaign dominated the local news in 1953 and 1954), which in turn inspired others to contribute $20 million to build Woodruff's new hospital. Dr. Kate also was the subject of a 1954 *This Is Your Life* TV show. Open mid-June through Labor Day, from 11 A.M. to 4:00 P.M., Monday through Friday. No fee, but donations are accepted.

Peck's Wildwood Wildlife Park. Woodruff. More like an outdoor classroom than those popular theme parks. Kids love this place because hundreds of tame animals roam throughout the grounds. When was the last time you petted a porcupine? Open May through October. $6.50 for adults, $4.50 for children. WI 70 West. (715) 356-5588.

Little Swiss Village. Minocqua. The extra effort to get here is worth the

Bosacki's Boat House

Begun in 1917 in a building built in 1896, this historic establishment has more to it than an interesting atmosphere. Since July 22, 1972, it has had an intriguing story to tell. That's when a boat exploded near the gas dock and caused a fire that destroyed the original building. Talk about fans. About 15,000 of them, some from as far away as Russia, took up the fight and circulated a petition urging the owners to rebuild. They did, of course, and the result is a comfortable spot on the lake with regulars coming from miles around for savory prime rib (if you like yours medium to well done, put in a strong request), steaks, fish, and burgers. Fourth-generation family members now run this venerable institution. Reservations don't come easy on Friday nights (when fish fries draw fans from all over) or on Wednesday, Friday, and Sunday nights in the summer when the Minocqua Bats perform their water-ski shows. Their ramp is not far from Bosacki's dock, so savvy diners ask for a table on the glass-enclosed porch to watch the show. Contributing to the activities are a marina, a bait-and-tackle shop, and a sweet shop. Located next to the bridge, on U.S. 51 in Minocqua. (715) 356-5292.

drive, which incidentally is a pleasant loop around beautiful Blue Lake. If you've been in the Black Forest of Germany or Switzerland, you'll feel right at home in this Bavarian homestead filled with flowers and chalets. This Swiss retreat, run by a fourth-generation Swiss family, offers more than just gazing at the inviting lakeside setting. Shop in the chalets, eat in the lodge, or stay awhile at the Gasthaus Motel. Polka music sets the mood for shopping the tiny Das Wald Haus. Here you'll find imports such as cuckoo clocks,

The Little Swiss Village—a Bavarian homestead near Minocqua—includes shops, lodging, and a restaurant.

Delftware, and Swiss chocolates. The Geneva Haus Boutique has striking fashions for men and women from around the world. The Swiss Miss Shoppe stocks a variety of unique gifts. Little Swiss Village doesn't pretend to have all the Swiss imports you'd ever want to find under one Wisconsin roof (for that you'll have to go to the southern part of the state to Robert's European Imports in New Glarus), but the atmosphere in this Swiss compound is A-plus. The restaurant overlooking the lake is open for breakfast, brunch, and lunch from 8 A.M. until 3 P.M. The village is open throughout the summer, so call ahead in spring and fall. Two and a half miles south of the Minocqua bridge on U.S. 51, then three miles west on Blue Lake Road. (715) 356-3675.

Northern Lights Playhouse. Hazelhurst. Features Broadway shows (both musicals and nonmusicals) and children's theater productions, with a top-notch cast of actors culled from pros across the country. Open June through

October. Daily performances with some matinees. (715) 356-7173.

Northland Historical Society Museum. This nicely presented museum has been preserving the past since 1957. Antique angling paraphernalia, old farm tools, and lots of logging and railroad items abound. No admission Open mid-June to September. About 10 miles south of Woodruff on WI 47 in Lake Tomahawk, then one block east to the Hoffman House. 7247 Kelly Drive. (715) 277-2602.

Scheer's Lumberjack Shows. Woodruff. All the lumberjack stuff you may have seen on TV—ax throwing, log rolling, tree climbing, canoe tumbling—it's all here in a North Woods—style carnival atmosphere. The "actors" are champion lumberjacks just doing what they do best. Open June through August. (715) 356-4050.

Snowshoe Baseball. That's right, baseball played on snowshoes. Where else are you going to see that but in the good old North Woods? These players show true grit—games held every Monday night at Lake Tomahawk's Athletic Field. Free admission. Late June through mid-August. One block west of WI 47, Lake Tomahawk. For more information call the Lake Tomahawk Information Bureau. (715) 277-2602.

Torpy Park and Public Beach. Minocqua. This small, picturesque park on the shores of Lake Minocqua (across from the New Concord Inn) is a couple of blocks from the downtown area. U.S. 51 runs one-way (south) along here, so walking across the highway is relatively safe. There's a lifeguard in attendance, a roped-off swimming area, and a small pier. Also an attractive stone and timber building adjacent to the park has changing

Watch Out for Deer

Be alert when you're driving in Wisconsin's North Woods. There are over 800,000 white-tailed deer living in the state's forests. It's fun to spot one munching leaves a few feet from your car, but it's no picnic if car and deer collide. In a recent year 350,000 deer were killed by automobiles. The white-tail is the state's number-one game animal, but it's also the number-one animal culprit when it comes to causing property damage.

How can you decrease the possibility of having a car-deer accident? Buckle up, don't drive close to the car in front of you, and tell your passengers to watch out for deer. One of the charms of the North Woods is their rugged isolation, but that also means you may spend part of your time driving on unlit roads at night. Car headlights usually scare deer into the woods, although they are also known to freeze in the glare. Occasionally they may become disoriented and abruptly dash into oncoming traffic. You can help prevent this by driving slower in dark areas so you can brake quickly if needed.

If you hit a deer, get your car off the road and report the accident to the local sheriff or police. For those who want to keep the carcass after the collision, it's legal to do so but only after it has been tagged by law officials.

rooms, showers, and terraces for stretching out and enjoying the view. Below, a nice pier with benches is a good place to sit and enjoy the continuous parade

The pier at Minocqua's beautiful Torpy Park.

of passing boats. Watch boaters as they maneuver from Minocqua Lake into the other six lakes that make up this chain.

Warbonnet Zoo. What is it about the North Woods and wild-animal parks? They seem to spring up wherever tourists gravitate. This one has more offerings than most and has year-round activities (call for winter hours). See exotic animals like Watusi cattle and lemur. Guided nature walks, safari rides, fall and winter hayrides, cross-country skiing, and snowshoeing all take place within the park's 50 acres. Consider a fall visit when hayrides take you through color-

Torpy Park pavilion with changing rooms and rest area.

ful woods. $4.50 for adults, $3.50 for children under 15. U.S. 51 in Hazelhurst. (715) 356-5093.

Wilderness Cruises. Hazelhurst. Take a ride on board the 76-foot *Wilderness Queen*, a comfortable cabin cruiser with an open-air top deck. You won't forget your adventure into the Willow Reservoir, a beautiful forested sanctuary covering 100,000 acres. Watch eagles soar while sipping champagne on the brunch tour. Other excursions include sunset dinner cruises and moonlight cruises. Basic cruises are $9 for adults, $6 for children. (715) 453-3310.

Lodging

You'll find everything from hotels and motels, to resorts, private homes, vacation homes, cottages, bed and breakfasts, and campgrounds. Check with the Minocqua-Arbor Vitae-Woodruff Chamber of Commerce for additional help. Here are a few notable accommodations.

HAZELHURST

Black's Cliff. The Black family built their family-oriented resort on lower Kaubashine Lake so their guests could have privacy along with magnificent lakeside views. These vacation homes all have large screened porches and new appliances, and some have fireplaces. Free fishing boat provided with each home. Motors rented by day or week. You can also rent paddleboats, pontoons, canoes, and a kayaks. (715) 356-3018.

MINOCQUA

Beacons. This legendary boathouse has been around since the turn of the century. When you're at Bosacki's Boat House (see accompanying description), you'll see the Beacons resort directly across the lake. Nightly or weekly rates with one- and two-bedroom units available. (715) 356-5515.

The Minocqua Inn. Bed and breakfast on seven acres not far from the Bearskin Trail. Your full breakfast includes Kona coffee and Hawaiian macadamia nut sweetbread, samples of the culinary expertise Dana and Ron McMullin gleaned during their Hawaiian days. Their inn features three rooms: The Rustic Room, The Aloha Room, and The Minocqua Room. (715) 358-2578.

The New Concord Inn. Located close to Woodruff and across the street from Torpy Park and Lake Minocqua, this inn has an urban feeling and is impeccably clean. Pine-paneled indoor pool and whirlpool. Complimentary continental breakfast in the conference room (yes, all those wildlife pictures on the walls are for sale) includes muffins, kringles, minibagels, juice, and coffee. (715) 356-1800 or (800) 356-8888.

The Pointe Resort Hotel and Conference Center. First-class resort on Lake Minocqua where you'll find tennis, boating, a swimming beach, indoor pool, sauna, and many other amenities. Balconies and patios come with each condominium suite. (715) 356-4431.

Wilson's Shishebogama Shores Resort. Five housekeeping cottages (three have three bedrooms, two have two bedrooms) along picturesque Lake Shishebogama. Kitchens fully equipped with everything you need. Secluded spot on quiet bay. Open year-round. (715) 356-5974.

Out to Eat

MINOCQUA

Back Bay Supper Club. Seven miles west of Minocqua on Highway 70 on Lake Shishebogama. The 30-ounce porterhouse steak and deep-fried or broiled walleye are house specialties. Seafood, steaks, and ribs are why those in the know flock here. Seven miles west on WI 70, on Lake Shishebogama. (715) 358-7818.

Bosacki's Boat House. See the accompanying description of this local institution—not to be missed.

Mama's. When you tire of supper club fare, head to Mama's, where Italian cooking reigns supreme. They've been cooking up old-time family recipes since the 1950s. Menu favorites include pizza, pasta primavera, mostaccioli, ravioli, veal Parmesan, and fettuccine Alfredo. American cuisine is also served. Three miles west on WI 70, on Curtis Lake. (715) 356-5070.

The Red Steer. Every size steak you've ever dreamed about. Veal, chicken, seafood, and fish are other offerings. Two blocks south of the Minocqua Bridge on U.S. 51. (715) 356-6332.

Dine like a lumberjack at Paul Bunyan's Cook Shanty.

WOODRUFF

Paul Bunyan's Cook Shanty. Don't worry about not being able to find this place. Since 1961, an immense Paul Bunyan and his blue ox Babe have been standing guard near the highway, adjacent to the cook shanty. Inside, the lumberjack atmosphere continues with taffy-colored log walls and ceilings, old lumberjack tools, and picnic tables spread with red and white tablecloths. Come by for Sunday dinner and you're likely to have 12 or more items served family-style, including fried and roasted chicken, roast sirloin, and a slew of accompaniments, including dessert and beverage, all for $10.95.

Lumberjack breakfasts, luncheons, and Friday night fish fries are also served. On U.S. 51, on the border of Minocqua and Woodruff. (715) 356-6270.

Shopping

Shopping is a favorite pastime in Minocqua. And not just for faraway visitors. Those who live in neighboring towns regularly make the trek. The Minocqua area has a potpourri of wearable art and livable fashions to fawn over. Word of these treasures has spread to other parts of the North Woods. Take Rebeccah, for instance, the front-desk receptionist at the Super 8 in Park Falls, about an hour away. When she learned I'd recently been in Minocqua, she became as animated and inquisitive as if I'd just returned from the Garment District in New York.

The best variety of shopping can be experienced in downtown Minocqua on **Main Street**. Many restored old buildings now double as galleries and gift shops.

Gaslight Square. On the first floor you'll find a mix of gifts and quality collectibles, including sporting goods, jewelry, soaps and potpourri, and locally made jams and jellies. Upstairs, browse through several rooms of antiques at Attic Antiques. In downtown Minocqua, just north of the bridge.

Old Depot Shops. Near Torpy Park in Minocqua, these shops sell a variety of collectibles and gifts.

Lac du Flambeau

Thirteen miles northwest of Woodruff, the city of Lac du Flambeau lies in the middle of the Lac du Flambeau Indian Reservation and in the vicinity of the area's chain of 10 lakes. The area became the permanent home of the Chippewa in 1745 because of its excellent fishing, hunting, and rice beds. The name Lac du Flambeau ("lake of the torches") came from early fishermen, who used torches to help locate their prey in the dark. **For additional information, call the Lac du Flambeau Chamber of Commerce, (715) 588-3346.**

Sights and Attractions

George W. Brown Jr., Ojibwa Museum and Culture Center. You'll learn about the Ojibwa's rich culture and heritage. Interesting and insightful exhibits. Open early May through late October. In downtown Lac du Flambeau. (715) 588-3333.

Indian Bowl Dancers. If you're in the area in July or August, come by the reservation's Indian Bowl on a Tuesday evening. You'll be treated to dancers creating traditional dances in full costume. In downtown Lac du Flambeau.

Lake of the Torches Resort Casino. An attractive northern-lodge atmosphere in the midst of a wooded setting offers splendid views of the adjacent Pokegama Lake. The nonstop (24-hours a day) casino features 650 slot machines, 24 blackjack tables, video poker, and more. Come for the day or stay awhile at the 103-room resort, which includes swimming, water sports, hiking, snowmobiling, a restaurant, and entertainment. (800) 25-TORCH.

Waswagoning Indian Village. You'll gain insight into the tribal customs of an authentic sixteenth-century village. Highlights include a maple sugar camp and demonstrations of rarely seen skills and crafts, such as canoe and wigwam building. A good place to learn and grow. West on WI 47 to County H, then a short distance to the village, adjacent to Moving Cloud Lake. Open Memorial Day through Labor Day. (715) 588-3560.

Boulder Junction

Boulder Junction traces its history to when trappers and traders made their way through the area in the late 1700s. But the first permanent residents didn't put down stakes until the late 1800s, when logging became big business. When the railroad arrived in 1903, the landscape, as if on cue, began to change. With it came a steady, albeit somewhat slow, growth of resorts. In 1927 the town incorporated and was named for the intersection of two prime lumber companies on Boulder Lake. Today, the town has about 1,000 permanent residents.

Luckily, Boulder Junction, 10 miles south of the Upper Michigan border, has escaped the strip mall building frenzy of other North Woods spots that many tourists flock to. Muskie fishing is the primary magnet for those making the trek to the area's pristine lakes. You won't see a lot of hoopla advertising theme parks or recreational activities. Instead, downtown Boulder Junction offers a few nice, rather upscale shops and a retreatlike atmosphere that appears untarnished and undiscovered. The townsfolk are friendly too. It almost seems they have nothing better to do than to make sure you have good memories about their chosen place.

Visitors who enjoy the woods and water find plenty to do here—far more than just angling. Boulder Junction is in the middle of the Northern Highland State Forest and boasts of having 194 lakes within nine miles of the town's center. More often than not, locals will tell you that visitors keep coming back to their same piece of paradise year after year. The Malmgrens, who own White Birch Village, a vacation resort in the state forest, are good examples of Boulder Junction's staying power. Carol Malmgren's family had been coming to Wilsie's White Birch Lodge (the resort's former name) every summer since the 1940s. When the resort came up for sale in the early 1980s, the Malmgrens bought it, keeping intact their tradition of spending time at the same place every summer (although now it's every spring, summer, and fall).

Things might be changing for Boulder Junction, although at last count, most tourists hadn't heard the news. In 1997 Sports Afield magazine named it one of the country's best outdoor sports towns. That translates to a place where prices are reasonable, people are friendly, sports and recreational pursuits are plentiful, and your dog and cat are welcome.

Sights and Attractions

B.A.T.S. That's the Boulder Junction Area Trail System. The DNR, in conjunction with the town of Boulder Junction, opened the town's first mountain-bike trail in 1995. A second loop opened in 1997, and more trails are in the planning stages. Hike, bike, and rollerblade around the area with the help of maps provided at the **Boulder Junction Chamber of Commerce. For more information call (715) 385-2400 or (800)-GO-MUSKY.**

Events

Muskie Jamboree and Arts and Crafts Fair. This annual mid-August celebration includes flea market, fun runs, brats, ice cream, bake sales, and over 150 arts and crafts exhibitors. In downtown Boulder Junction. For more information contact the Chamber of Commerce.

Northern Highland Distance Ride. If you've never heard of endurance riding, then show up here and learn more about it. Anyone who has a horse is welcome to compete in cross-country rides of 15, 25, and 50 miles. Horses and riders make their way along marked snowmobile and ski trails and old logging roads. In late August, beginning at the Boulder Junction Community Center.

Lodging

Boulder Junction has a large assortment of accommodations ranging from vacation home rentals to rustic cottages. Here's a sampling of the variety.

Boulder Bear Motor Lodge. New log lodge, with a close-in location, 20 rooms, deer-viewing rooms, whirlpool, restaurant, and fish freezing facilities. Continental breakfast included. Restful atmosphere. 5437 County M. (715) 385-2662.

The Eagles Nest. Two secluded cottages, yet not far from town on Middle Gresham Lake. The draw is the peaceful location, outstanding panfishing, and wildlife viewing. Boats, canoes, and paddleboats are part of the experience. 4408 Middle Gresham Lane. (715) 385-2802.

Pap-Qua. This 100-year-old estate on Trout Lake includes 300-year-old virgin pines and a private island for guests' use. Housekeeping cabins feature TVs, VCRs, microwaves, and grills. 3552 Rocky Reef Lane. (715) 356-5352.

Volinek's Upper Gresham Resort. Good swimming spot on Upper Gresham Lake, with pier and raft. Accessibility to great fishing spots on chain of three lakes. Boats, motors, paddleboats, canoes available. Open year-round. 4480 U.S. 51 North. (715) 385-2578.

White Birch Village. A venerable North Woods institution. Eleven beautifully appointed vacation homes with imaginative touches, some with fireplaces. Family spot features a nice sandy beach for swimming, with a playground nearby and a variety of boats available. Boating and fishing on crystal-clear and muskie-laden White Birch Lake, on a three-lake chain. There's also a separate building for relaxing in a whirlpool and spa. (715) 385-2182.

Out to Eat

Boulder Beer Bar and Restaurant. What better place to knock down a wine cooler or beer than at a place that looks like it came straight out of Northern Exposure. Pizza, pasta, and other hearty foods are served. Wash your meal down with one of 300 beers available. On Main Street. (715) 385-2749.

Guide's Inn. Savory choices include seafood, German, and Italian entrees, as well as fine Continental cuisine. At the corner of Center Street and County M. (715) 385-2233.

Shopping

The Blueberry Patch. Country store features sweaters, jewelry, furniture, European lace, and lots of North Woods finds. 10351 Main Street. (715) 385-2142.

Bill Sherer's We Tie It. I like places that don't mince words. Here they tell you exactly what they do—and they do it well: custom-built rods, rod repair, everything you want to know about fly-tying. Seminars, classes, and a guide service available. Downtown Boulder Junction. (715) 385-0171.

Coontail Sports. Not a sports bar or restaurant, this gathering place is jam packed with sporting goods—everything from kayaks and canoes to cross-country skis and snowshoes. Adjacent to Coontail Corner, in downtown Boulder Junction, 5466 Park Street. (715) 385-0250.

Boulder Junction Marketplace. Diverse market features homemade sausage, bacon, hams, and many other specialty foods. Their motto: "You all come see us." Downtown Boulder Junction. (715) 385-2481.

Skids. Moccasins, sweatshirts, gifts galore. Just off Main Street on County M. (715) 385-2076.

Manitowish and Manitowish Waters

Each year Wisconsin's cranberry marshes produce approximately 30 percent of the country's cranberry crop. And near the twin towns of Manitowish and Manitowish Waters, cranberry bogs bordering the Little Trout and Alder Lakes have earned the distinct honor of being the country's most productive.

In addition to cranberries, the area is also known for its infamous connection with gangster John Dillinger. On U.S. 51 just south of Manitowish Waters, look for **Little Bohemia Lodge**. Back in 1934 the FBI received a tip that several suspicious guests were staying at the lodge's cabins. On a cold April day agents started out from Rhinelander to track down John Dillinger and "Baby Face" Nelson. The agents arrived at Little Bohemia with some of them standing on the cars' running boards, since two of the agents' cars had broken down en route. Their plan of attack backfired, however. Nelson was already holding two local men at gunpoint. The ensuing gunfight resulted in the death of Special Agent W. Carter Baum and the wounding of two other agents. Amidst the gunfire, Nelson and Dillinger escaped. Little Bohemia had become a household word.

Manitowish Waters' log post office fits the North Woods landscape.

For those interested in the follow-up, a few months later, in July 1934, Dillinger was shot to death by federal agents when he came out of the Biograph Theater in Chicago after seeing Clark Gable in Manhattan Melodrama; the agents had been tipped off by Dillinger's female companion. Nelson met his end in November of the same year, heralding the beginning of the end of the gangster era.

A multitude of gangster memorabilia is on display at Little Bohemia—the lodge is still going strong and serves dinner from early spring through early winter, with lunches only in the summer. For the more curious, the gangster's hideout cabin is on Little Star Lake.

Sights and Attractions

Cranberry Colorama Harvest and Festival. The end of September marks the beginning of the annual cranberry harvest. Event includes a flea market, a muskie-and-wild-rice dinner, games, more food, free pontoon-boat rides, and tours of the local cranberry marshes. Craft shows and flea markets are usually held next to the Community Building on U.S. 51. **For dates and specific events contact the Manitowish Waters Chamber of Commerce, (715) 543-8488.**

Cranberry Marsh Tours. Start at the heart of Manitowish Waters at the Community Center. Watch a video, sip cranberry juice, nibble on "craisens" (dried cranberries), then follow your guide via car to the marshes. Open mid-July through October. Free of charge. (715) 543-8488.

Lodging

Aberdeen Lodge. New first-class log lodge with many amenities. Good location for swimming, boating, fishing, and other water activities. Located on 100 acres along Manitowish's chain of 14 lakes. The main lodge has a dining room, bar, lounge, and gift shop. Log cottages have fully equipped kitchens, daily housekeeping, and range in size from two to four bedrooms. There's also a honeymoon log cottage with a fireplace and whirlpool in the master bedroom. Twin Pines Road. Open year-round. (715) 543-8700.

Pea Patch Motel and Saloon. Talk about diversity. It's a motel (5 rooms), restaurant, and saloon, all rolled into one. Die-hard peanut fans come by on Saturdays to throw peanut shells on the floor. Honest! Billed as the "Best Motel and Saloon by a Dam Site." On County W. (715) 543-2455.

Timberline Inn. New, beautiful log building in the heart of teeny Manitowish Waters. Twenty rooms, complimentary continental breakfast. (715) 543-8080.

Decorative log sign greets guests at the Timberline Inn.

Out to Eat

Michaels Bakery and Parlor and Restaurant. This attractive in-the-woods restaurant on the right as you're traveling north on U.S. 51, is open year-round. Popular gathering spot features many different cranberry concoctions. You'll find it on U.S. 51 (715) 543-2550.

Swanberg's Bavarian Inn. Features hearty German dishes served in comfortable surroundings. Another of those North Woods traditions—this one has catered to loyal patrons for over 50 years. (715) 543-2122.

Shopping

Northern Gear. Next door to the Timberline Inn, this shop is filled with great North Woods gifts (they carry birch wastebaskets, but these don't look like souvenirs), sports accessories, and clothes for men and women. You'd swear you're shopping on the North Shore of Chicago. (715) 543-8050.

Pepper's Place. For more shopping, take a few strides from Northern Gear and explore this nicely stocked log gift shop. Across from another log building—the Manitowish Post Office.

Mercer

This is a town with a sense of humor. Its residents love loons so much, they call Mercer the Loon Capital of Wisconsin, and in 1981 they built a 16-foot, 2,000-pound loon next to the Chamber of Commerce that is hard to miss. (What is it about the North Woods and monstrous memorials and shrines: Paul Bunyan and his blue ox, Babe, the mammoth muskie in Hayward, and the loon?) What a wake-up call to the fact that you've arrived in loon country.

Save the answer to this question in case you go on Jeopardy: Where was Smoky the Bear created? You guessed it. In 1950, he originated right here in Mercer when the local forest rangers came up with the idea and image. Curiosity seekers can see Smoky's outfit at the Mercer Ranger Station on State House Road, just north of town.

Mercer has other claims to fame besides loons and bears. In the late 1800s, tourists began flocking into area resorts once the Milwaukee, Lake Shore, and Western Railroad officially opened the area to more visitors. Regional residents had already discovered the area, and summer homes built by Hurley and Ironwood folks began springing up.

Mercer was also put on the map because of the Capone brothers, Al, George, Ralph, and Matt. They gravitated to the Jack Salome Lodge, spending many vacations fishing and relaxing. Ralph, though, decided he couldn't get enough of Mercer, so he stayed on, living in the area for many years and enjoying a reputation as well-respected citizen.

Once bustling with tourists, the Mercer area has, for the last couple of decades, been a quiet resting spot for those who want to get away from typical tourist hot spots. However, in 1990 the Department of Natural Resources bought the pristine Turtle Flambeau Flowage, comprising some 200 lakes. The fact that it's a mere 20 minutes from Mercer is a plus for those wanting to bring more visitors into the area.

Those who love ATVs have already discovered the Mercer area. These sports enthusiasts consider this destination as one of the best trail-riding spots in the country. **For more information, call the Mercer Chamber of Commerce, (715) 476-2389. For snow and winter trail conditions, call (715) 476-SNOW.**

Sights and Attractions

Lake of the Falls. Fishing hot spot consists of 338 acres and 25 feet deep, filled with walleye, northern pike, smallmouth bass, and muskie. Just north of Mercer, turn onto County FF, then go about three miles.

The Pines and Mines Mountain Bike Trail System. Over 300 miles of mapped and marked trails weave in and out of Iron County's most scenic splendor. Some trails take you through the Ottawa National Forest, affording breathtaking views of waterfalls and lakes.

Events

Loon Day Craft Fair. If you're around Mercer the first week of August (the fair is usually held the first Wednesday of each August), take in the work of local artisans. For more information, call (715) 476-2389.

Lodging

Deadhorse Lodge. Talk about sounding like a last outpost, it's hard to beat this name. Located in the Turtle Flambeau Flowage, these vacation homes let you enjoy the wild beauty of the woods around you. Superb fishing and snowmobiling nearby. Open year-round. (715) 476-2521.

Great Northern Motel. The name says it all. This is a motel with great perks, such as a swimming pool, whirlpool, continental breakfast, and great room for gathering around the fireplace. Located on a prime snowmobile trail, south on U.S. 51. (715) 476-2440.

Musky Point Resort. Water, water, water everywhere. A lot of it converges around here, with this resort at the center of it all. Open year-round, the cabins are located on Lake of the Falls, Turtle River, Moose Creek, Dollar Creek, and Three Black Lakes. As if that weren't enough water, these lakes combine with the Turtle Flambeau Flowage. 4946N Musky Point Road. (715) 476-2175.

Voyageur Inn. Historic pub and lodge tucked away off the beaten track. Rooms in the lodge or housekeeping cabins. Solitude and beauty five miles from Mercer, on Lake of the Falls. Open year-round. (715) 476-0013.

Out to Eat

Anchor Inn. If you're on a snowmobile, you can't beat the location for eating on the run—a snowmobile trail is adjacent to the parking lot. Famous for hearty fare, including good soups and chili. U.S. 51, downtown. (715) 476-2251.

Ullman's Ding-A-Ling Supper Club. One of the area's most popular spots for winding down and eating well-prepared chicken, ribs, seafood, and steak. At the intersection of U.S. 51 and WI 47, three miles south. (715) 476-2270.

The Hideaway. Lodge rooms and cottages are available, but those in the know come here for good eats, including Friday night fish fries. Located on the scenic Turtle Flambeau Flowage. Open year-round. 2139 Popko Circle West. (715) 476-2160.

Skip and Lynn's Around the Corner Pub. Chicken, fish, and burgers are the favorites here, with chicken being the biggest draw—broasted, fried, you name it, they've probably got it. Closed Mondays. Railroad Street. (715) 476-2472.

Tom's Country Cafe. Popular spot to hang out in downtown Mercer. Homemade soups, pies, and all the fixings. U.S. 51. (715) 476-2433.

Hurley

There's no doubt about it. Hurley looks weathered. And it still feels like a frontier town that has seen a lot of salty, raucous living. Early loggers and miners were warned that the four wildest places on earth were Cumberland, Hell, Hurley, and Hayward. Hurley, though, had the reputation of being the wickedest.

There were hundreds of mines in the nearby Gogebic and Penokee Iron Ranges a century ago, along with the countless logging operations. And so saloons and bootleg-liquor operations sprang up in Hurley, all in the name of accommodating the deluge of overworked miners and lumberjacks looking for fun. Hurley's history includes its "lower block"—rows and rows of buildings where bootleg operations went on. The sleeping quarters above gave a whole new meaning to "sleeping above the store."

But it's Silver Street that fascinates most visitors. As late as the 1970s, this strip of a few blocks was the town's

South of Hurley, on Highway 51, is this distinctive Vietnam Veterans War Memorial.

lusty center, packed with saloons tempting customers with exotic dancers and strip shows. Today a few clubs still operate, purportedly within the town's laws, and many taverns look like they're prospering. But Silver Street's checkered past and reputation as being tough as nails has softened. Today you're more likely to blend in with other visitors walking or driving down Silver Street trying to get a glimpse of the past. **Hurley Area Chamber of Commerce. Silver Street. (715) 561-4334.**

Sights and Attractions

Cross-Country Skiing. Numerous cross-country ski trails provide unsurpassed scenic beauty. The Montreal Trail can accommodate skiers of all levels and abilities, and it provides interesting sights such as the old Montreal Mining Operation. The Uller Trail pivots and turns through the Penokee

61

Range for over 17 miles, ending in Montreal. For maps of these and other cross-country ski trails, contact the Iron County Development Zone, (715) 561-2922.

Downhill Skiing. Iron County is the gateway to some of the Midwest's finest skiing—including Whitecap Mountain, Wisconsin's largest downhill-ski operation. Within 10 miles of the Iron County border you'll find Big Powderhorn Mountain, Blackjack Mountain, and Indianhead Mountain in Michigan.

Iron County Historical Museum. This impressive old brownstone, with its towers and turrets, is now a colorful clearinghouse of Iron County history. Don't miss one of the more unusual first-floor exhibits. You'll find local

residents using large looms made by early settlers to weave various products, such as rugs. In addition to do-nations, money from the sale of these products is a major source of museum funding. Among other exhibits on the second floor, you'll see how the courthouse clock, high in the clock tower, works. The tower has been home to the clock since 1893, but it wasn't electrified until 1922. If you have the stomach for it, go down to the museum's basement to check out the morgue. There's a tin casket, cooling board, and altar on display. The same basement contains other items, including wine-making equipment, old washing ma-chines, and farm tools. A fascinating mix of memorabilia not often found in country historical museums. Open Monday, Wednesday, Friday, and Saturday. 303 Iron Street. (715) 561-2244.

High on a hill on Hurley's Iron Street is the impressive Iron County Historical Museum, once the Iron County Courthouse.

Waterfalls. This is waterfall country. In fact, Iron County has more waterfalls than any other Wisconsin county. As the seasons change, waterfalls take on the look of the season. Visit them year-round for dramatically different characteristics. Two area examples are: Potato River Falls, which cascade over 90 feet. Take U.S. 2 west of Hurley for about 18 miles to WI 169, turn left and go through

Gurney, then head west on Potato River Falls Road for a mile and a-half.

Peterson Falls. This beauty on the east branch of the Montreal River falls 35 feet. Take U.S. 2 west of Hurley for a half mile to an unpaved road. Stay on this road and go directly east—don't take any other turns. When you get to a small turnaround area, park and walk about one-quarter mile to the falls. Or simply follow the sound of rushing water.

The Wisconsin Travel Information Center. More than a typical wayside visitors' center, this attractive facility is a good place to stop, unwind, and

North of Hurley, on Highway 51, visitors can relax and gather information about the area at the Wisconsin Travel Information Center.

glean useful information about the area. And, if you've been following U.S. 51 through northern Wisconsin, make this a mandatory stop—you can then say you've reached the end of Highway 51. This visitor center is packed with useful guides and maps, plus it's an attractive mini-museum in disguise. It has large pink granite rock that doubles as a water fountain, and the old mining memorabilia is worth a stop. North of town near the Days Inn. (715) 561-5310.

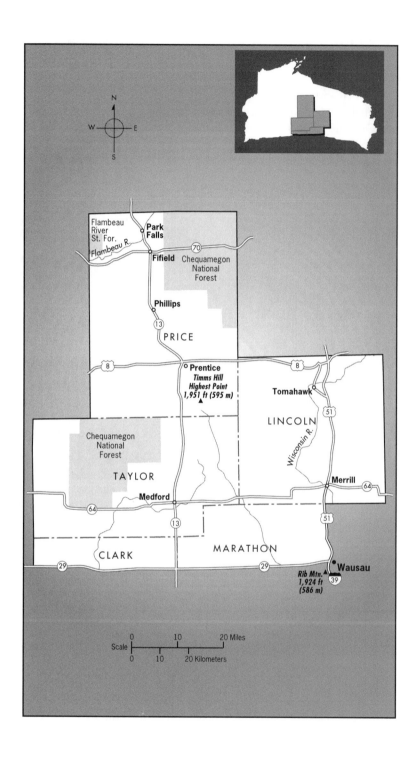

N

W · E

S

Flambeau
River
St. For.
Flambeau R.

Park
Falls

Fifield

70

Chequamegon
National
Forest

Phillips

13

PRICE

8

Prentice
*Timms Hill
Highest Point
1,951 ft (595 m)* ▲

8

Tomahawk

51

LINCOLN

Chequamegon
National
Forest

TAYLOR

Wisconsin R.

Merrill

64

Medford

64

13

51

CLARK

MARATHON

29

29

Rib Mtn. ▲
*1,924 ft
(586 m)*

Wausau

39

Scale

0   10   20 Miles

0   10   20 Kilometers

chapter 3
the West Central Woods

There's an unpretentiousness to this portion of the North Woods that starts near Tomahawk, in Lincoln County, then continues on to Park Falls, in the northwest portion of Price County, and then farther up to Butternut. You won't see endless shopping malls, arcades, and theme parks in this section of the North Woods, but when you meander off the main roads, you'll see endless tunnels of trees and simple, yet stunning scenery.

There's an uncommercialized atmosphere in this land of bald eagles, black bear, ruffed grouse, and trophy deer. Many visitors come to see the blaze of colors in the fall. For camera buffs, there are endless "best-woods-and-waters" spots. For the height of dramatic backdrops, come in autumn when the landscape is lit up with streamers of brilliant orange, yellow, and red.

Many of the area's towns, such as Fifield and Phillips, were once booming lumber centers during the late 1800s. But once the last stands of magnificent pine forests were felled and the boom towns turned to bust, the towns that survived did so by reinventing themselves. Park Falls, for instance, attracted forest-products industries, Fifield's cranberry bogs brought in new business, and Tomahawk began building motorcycles at the Harley-Davidson plant.

It's probably fair to say that most visitors who seek out this section of Wisconsin are not as much interested in its towns as they are in the area's mighty forests and rugged wilderness. This is an outdoor sports paradise. Hunters, anglers, cross-country skiers, ATV riders, snowmobile riders, and boaters find this a powerfully hypnotic place for unwinding and having fun.

Outdoor playgrounds are mighty impressive in these parts. You can enjoy a variety of sports throughout the year in the massive Chequamegon National Forest, the Flambeau River State Forest, and the wild Turtle Flambeau Flowage. Thousands of acres of unspoiled wilderness are at your disposable. You'll never absorb it all in one visit because the area has such a broad expanse of lakes, rivers, rapids, and tunnels of trees.

Woods and water are undeniably the big attraction up here, so much so that visitors who fall under the area's spell tend to keep coming back. Repeat visitors are numerous in these sections—so common in fact that resorts like Boyd's Mason Lake Resort in Fifield have acknowledged the loyalty of turn-of-the-century lodgers who repeatedly stayed there by naming cabins after them.

Serious escapism is, after all, in keeping with the spirit of the great outdoors.

If you've enjoyed hiking or biking the trails in summer, come back during another season. Nature's many moods can easily be explored here. Enjoy gentle breezes off Sailor Lake in the Chequamegon, or lazy fishing off the shores of the Pike Lake chain. If you tire of placid lakes, hook up with a canoe outfitter like the Oxbo Resort in Park Falls (they've been overseeing canoe adventures since 1922). You'll experience great canoeing on the Flambeau River's water trail, one of the North Woods's best-kept secrets.

Pumpkin patch on the way up north.

Tomahawk

A few miles west of U.S. 51 the North Woods scenery starts taking shape. There are no gigantic forests left here—early logging took care of that. But the area is rife with lakes and escapist feelings. Lake Tomahawk, named because of its resemblance to the axlike implement, is a fishing and boating destination. Several other lakes dot the area. Tomahawk grew up around the Wisconsin River, the city's main waterway. **For more information contact the Tomahawk Chamber of Commerce, (715) 453-5334 or (800) 569-2160.**

Sights and Attractions

Chapel on the Hill. Just a few miles south of Tomahawk on U.S. 51 in Irma, you can't help but notice a white clapboard church set in a magnificent glen off the highway in the Fort Hamilton complex. Is it a church or . . . an opportunity to stop and shop? The answer is both. You can get married here in a nondenominational wedding or stock up on antiques and old-fashioned general store merchandise. (715) 539-2810.

The Old Homestead Llama Farm. This is not a restaurant, but a highly unusual opportunity to take a hike with llamas and have lunch in the country. Billed as "Take a Llama to Lunch," your outing starts at the farm about 10 miles north of Tomahawk (call for directions). You'll hike along the trails of the Pinewood Country Club (in addition to golf, the club features vacation homes, a dinner theater, restaurant, and airport), a trek of one and a half hours each way. The club puts together a hearty lunch. Llama outings offered June through September, depending on the weather. 3197 Lakewood Road, off U.S. 51. (715) 453-3094.

Events

Kwahamot Water Ski Shows. The Kwahamot skiers (Kwahamot is Tomahawk spelled backwards) perform their stunts every Saturday, Tuesday, and Thursday on the Wisconsin River next to the Business U.S. 51 Bridge in Tomahawk. No charge. Shows run from June through September.

Lincoln County Rodeo Days. Participants in the Professional Rodeo Cowboys Association show off their skills in events such as bareback and bull riding. Usually the last weekend in June. Twenty miles south at the Lincoln County Fairgrounds in Merrill. (715) 536-2235.

Colorama Motocycle Ride. Sponsored by the Harley-Davidson plant in Tomahawk and the North Country Riders, this mid-September weekend event is full of pizzazz. Lots of activities including a downtown street dance and free Harley rides. (800) 645-RIDE.

Yesterfest. This is a big weekend-long festival with nonstop entertainment: bands and more bands, historical reenactments, food, history, antiques, and lumberjack shows. Usually the second week in August. At the Sara Park Activity Center, Tomahawk. For more information call the Tomahawk Chamber of Commerce, (715) 453-5334 or (800) 569-2160.

Lodging

The Bridge Inn. Located at Tomahawk's bridge, this attractive inn features rooms with Wisconsin River views. No need to go anywhere else to take in the waterfront activities. On Business U.S. 51. (715) 453-5323.

Duck Point Resort. Several modern lakeside cottages and vacation homes with names like Eider, Woodbuck, and Pintail are available with one to four bedrooms. Sandy beach, water slide, playgrounds, boat rentals are available. W5930 Duck Point Road. (800) 729-3489.

Super 8 Motel. Relax in the indoor pool or whirlpool. Or pamper yourself and ask for a room with its own whirlpool. Complimentary breakfast. Convenient location at the corner of Mohawk and Business U.S. 51. (715) 453-5210.

Out to Eat

Big Moose Inn. All-you-can-eat specials, prime rib, chicken, popular Friday fish fries, and a bountiful Sunday champagne brunch. Open at 4 P.M.

Business 51 in Tomahawk. (715) 453-6667.

Prime Time Restaurant and Lounge. Used to be the Matador restaurant. This wildly popular place experienced extensive fire damage in January of 1998 then underwent nearly a year of restoration. Worth the wait. They serve a popular Mexican menu and, back by popular demand, their all-time favorite lunch, breakfast, and dinner buffets, offered at various times during the week. Plus, there are many choices of down-home cooking. Next to the Super 8 Motel on U.S. 51 North. (715) 453-5885.

Prentice

Less than 40 miles west of Tomahawk is Prentice, population 570, near the intersection of U.S. 8 and WI 13. It's a "main street" sort of place—it even has a Main Street Cafe that serves above-average coffee. If you're traveling by car, Prentice is a good place to stop and unwind. Its pretty little park, on the South Fork of the Jump River, has a small picnic area, good views of the river, and, at one end of the shore, an American flag made from stones. Above the park, on the hill on Cherry Street, the historic First Baptist Church adds to the town's vintage ambiance.

Historic First Baptist Church in Prentice.

Eighteen miles southeast of Prentice, and east of Ogema, where County C and WI 86 connect, you'll come to **Timm's Hill County Par**k bordered by two spring-fed lakes. The main attraction here is the knoll at the top of the park—the highest geographical point in Wisconsin at 1951.5 feet above sea level. For panoramic views, climb the observation tower to see magnificent forests of ash, birch, maple, and basswood. Fall is the best time to make the climb and take in the 360 degrees of splendid colors. Hiking and ski trails also snake their way through the park. For those wanting to connect with the famous Ice Age Trail, you can hook up with it via the Timm's Hill Trail.

Phillips

Locals in Phillips, in an area chock full of lakes and rivers, like to remind you that when you've arrived there, you are no longer on your way to the North Woods, you are there. Located about 12 miles north of Prentice on WI 13, this spot in Price County is an ideal outdoor recreation destination. In the fall and winter, hunters move into the woods to track down deer, bear, and small game. Groomed snowmobile trails encompassing more than 500 miles and an abundance of well-groomed cross-country ski trails provide the backdrop for winter recreation. ATV riding is at its best here. For those crazy about water sports, the landscape is dotted with ice fishermen in the winter, and canoeists and water-skiers in the spring and summer.

Phillips's most famous attraction has nothing to do with outdoor sports, however. This is the nothing-like-it **Wisconsin Concrete Park**, south of town, on the right side of WI 13 as you're heading north. If you're not looking for this anachronism in the woods, it's easy to miss. Many motorists probably see the odd stone statues behind the fence on the highway, then whisk right by. Despite the

Folk artist Fred Smith's extraordinary cement and glass figures fill the nothing-like-it Wisconsin Concrete Park at Phillips.

sign announcing "Wisconsin Concrete Park," it won't mean much to the uninformed. If that describes you, you may miss one of Wisconsin's most unique collections of folk art and also the world's largest collection of art created from concrete.

It was 1950 when Fred Smith, native Phillips resident and 65-year-old lumberjack, musician, saloon owner, and farmer, started building life-size statues. Smith, a self-taught artisan, started by constructing wooden frames, then tying them together with mink wire. Next, he covered each frame with cement, then decorated each piece of art with dazzling fragments of clear and colored glass, old beer bottles, shells, and other odd ingredients. Smith worked furiously, building more than 200 characters before he died in 1976. Shortly after his death, the Kohler Foundation purchased the property, then donated it to Price County for use as a park.

Many characters are easy to recognize, such as Paul Bunyan, Sacajawea, and Ben Hur. Others statues stand and stare, while their counterparts engage in activities such as driving beer wagons. It's eerie walking through the park filled with groups of stone people. There's a haunting feeling that at some point, maybe after dark, they'll come alive and gossip about the strange tourists they saw that day.

When you're walking the grounds, take a look at the sign on the big garage by the parking lot. This was once Smith's barn where he held musical events in his "bandstand." Local musicians congregated here, along with Smith, who joined the revelry, often with bells strapped to his feet. The whole operation is cared for by Friends of Fred Smith, Inc., and the Price County Forestry Department, (715) 339-6371.

Next to the park is the Gallery and Gifts Shop in the Fred Smith House. Open May 28–December 24, the gallery represents many local artists whose work includes wood sculpture, pottery, stained glass, wearable art, fabric and fiber art, wildlife art, and much more. (715) 339-6475.

Events

Phillips Czechoslovakian Festival. Usually the third weekend in June, the festival celebrates the community's Czech heritage with cultural booths, crafts, logging displays, railroad exhibits, and more.

Yesterfest. Usually the second weekend in August. The displays include farm equipment and depictions of early life on the farm. Other nonstop entertainment often includes bands and more bands, lumberjack shows, food, antiques, and historical reenactments.

Visit or call the Price County Tourism Department, 126 Cherry Street, Phillips, for more information on these and other festivals, (715) 339-4505 or (800) 269-4505.

Flambeau River State Forest and Other Wilderness Areas

One of the state's seven state forests, the Flambeau River State Forest, located west of Phillips, has something for everyone. The river takes it name from the flambeau, a flaming torch used by early Native Americans to help them spear fish at night. The conservationists who, back in the early 1900s, began the initial stages of preservation in the area would be proud today. They started out determined to preserve 3,600 acres of wooded land—now the area consists of 90,000 acres of protected forest. (The forest was officially established in 1930.)

What can you do in the forest? For starters, this is prime white-water river country. The multiuse wilderness area is open year-round and has many lakes and cross-country and snowmobile trails. For camping experiences on large lakes, choose the Connor Lake Campground or the Lake of the Pines Campground. The Oxbo Ski Trail offers trails for novices as well as experts. You can explore about 55 miles of hiking trails and snowmobile trails, covering old logging roads and railroad corridors, along the North and South Forks of the Flambeau. There are also 14 miles of bike and hiking trails and 38 miles of ATV trails. **For more information about any of the area's facilities, contact Flambeau River State Forest, (715) 332-5271.**

The North Fork of the Flambeau River, a fast-water area, lies between Park Falls and the Flambeau River State Forest. Generally speaking, depending upon rainfall and the time of year, the river's northernmost parts are more leisurely, its southern sections more flamboyant and roaring. The section between Park Falls and the Turtle Flambeau Flowage is particularly challenging. Designated as the Upper Flambeau River Natural Area, this portion takes you through 23 rapids. Many resorts along the Flambeau's path cater to river rafting and canoeing—ask about shuttle services. One longtime reliable spot is the Oxbo Resort outside Park Falls. It offers

ATV Riding

In Price County, all-terrain vehicles (ATVs) are a common sight—on the highways being transported to the back woods, in restaurant and motel parking lots, and on the many trails themselves. The allure is the area's multitude of trails and good connecting roads. Many ATV riders gravitate to the area because of the Flambeau Trail System in the Chequamegon National Forest. The 60-mile system is sprinkled with wooden bridges, glistening lakes, bogs, and hilly terrain.

While some of the area's trail systems are out in the boonies, others are not far from restaurants and inns. The area is so ATV friendly that Park Falls even allows ATV riders to drive on designated city streets between April 15 and November 15 so they can get to inns, restaurants, and the like. There are four trails that offer good off-road rides in the area: The Flambeau Trail System, The Flambeau River State Forest Trail, The Tuscobia-Park Falls State Trail, and the Pine Line Trail. For more information call the Park Falls Area Chamber of Commerce, (715) 762-2703 or (800) 762-2709, or the Park Falls Service Center, (715) 762-3204. In Park Falls, stop at the USDA Forest Service for maps. For sales, rentals, and service call East Towne Recreational in Park Falls, (715) 762-3922 or (800) EST-TOWN.

71

two- and four-hour canoe trips, along with two- and three-day trips; call (715) 762-4786.

A fishing and hunting paradise, the South Fork winds its way from the Pike Lake chain, through the vast woods of the Chequamegon National Forest, then through Fifield and Lugerville. Anglers fish the South Fork for smallmouth bass, muskie, northern, walleye, and lake sturgeon. The area is also a draw for bear, deer, duck, grouse, and rabbit hunting.

Northwest of Park Falls, the Turtle Flambeau Flowage is a pristine wilderness area often compared to the Boundary Waters because of its raw beauty. Often referred to as The Crown Jewel of the North, this immense area has 19,000 lakes within its perimeters. There are more eagles, loons, and osprey pairs here than anywhere else in the state. Fall is a choice time to amble the woods, when Mother Nature's colors are at their most intense.

Fifield

Fourteen miles north of Phillips and three miles south of Park Falls on WI 13, you'll come to Fifield, once home base to hundreds of logging camps on the Flambeau and Elk Rivers. Now this small, unincorporated town's biggest industry is the Northland Cranberry Company outside of town.

The Fifield Town Hall Museum is a treasure trove of area memorabilia.

Sights and Attractions

Old Town Hall Museum. This restored 1894 building now serves as the town's museum. If the building looks ancient compared to the rest of Fifield (with the exception of the post office built in the early 1900s across the street) that's because the business district of Fifield burned down in a horrible fire in 1893. Listed on the National Register of Historic Places, it's worth a stop. Nicely displayed exhibits offer insight into the area during its logging camp heyday, from 1879 through the 1930s. There are logging tools and railroad memorabilia galore. Plus, there are several rooms of Victorian and turn-of-the-century accessories and artifacts, including an uncomfortable-looking red velvet dental chair from a Park Falls dentist, a needlepoint pillow depicting a woodland and water scene—stitched letters spell out "Where The Pines And Balsam Murmur"—and an old green knit bathing suit that looks as good as new. No admission but donations are appreciated. Open June through Labor Day, Fridays and Sundays only, 1:00 to 5:00 P.M. In the middle of town on WI 13. For more information, call the Park Falls Chamber of Commerce, (715) 762-2703.

Hick's Landing. More than a restaurant, more than a bar, Hick's is located in a gorgeous setting on Sailor Creek Flowage (locals say "crick") close to the Chequamegon National Forest. The casual atmosphere in the bar (this is a blue-jeans crowd) sets the tone for the entire operation. Dance-hall-like chairs lined against the wall hold anxious diners waiting for a table. The decor is ho-hum, a 1950s atmosphere caught in a time warp. Black vinyl bar stools and tired putty-colored linoleum are evident, but all that fades when you meet the personable Erma Hicks, the establishment's owner since 1951.

Sailor Creek Flowage near Fifield.

Erma and her husband (now deceased) moved from Milwaukee, cleared the land, and started their boat rental business with a tin can on a pier. Eventually, they added a beer garden, then expanded the restaurant three times over the years. Erma is part of the restaurant's appeal. She greets everyone as if they were a personal friend.

The appetizer tray is bigger and better than those found in most other supper clubs, one of the reasons being the tiny ramekins of baked beans. Piping-hot bread served on its own board is a personal touch. Most diners come for the steaks, lobsters, and burgers. (Be advised that the menu warns, "We do not recommend a well-done steak.") Try Erma's famous cranberry cake with hot brandy sauce for dessert—made with cranberries from the marsh down the road. Hick's Landing also rents out campground space and cabins, and offers

73

hunting, fishing, and snowmobiling. The restaurant is open Tuesday through Saturday from 5:00 P.M. (Sunday from 12:00 P.M.). One and a-half miles east of Fifield on WI 70, then three and a-half miles south on Hicks Road. Look for signs. (715) 762-5008.

Lodging

Boyd's Mason Lake Resort. One of the North Woods's most interesting and expansive resorts (on an enormous 2,600 acres), this vacation spot features 17 cabins on the shores of four lakes. Some of the cabins (forget the tiny cabin in the woods idea—some of these dwellings are four-bedroom homes) are named for vacationers who frequented Boyd's in the early 1900s. The main dining hall serves all-you-can-eat meals. Activities galore, with a playground, recreation building, boat rentals, and bike rentals. Open mid-May to mid-October. N12351 Boyd's Road, Fifield. (715) 762-3469.

Out to Eat

Northwoods Supper Club. You can't miss this one. It's at the intersection of WI 13 and WI 70 in the heart of Fifield—just look for the enormous fake deer on the front lawn. A long-time favorite spot for prime rib, steak, and shrimp. And, believe it or not, they feature not-often-found beef Wellington. (715) 762-4447.

Park Falls

There's something about driving into Park Falls, the largest town (population about 3,100) in the area, that gets you into the mood of the great outdoors. Maybe it's Park Falls's AM-radio station, WNBI 980, that plays pure golden oldies. Whatever the reason for the good vibes, Park Falls just happens to be a real down-home, friendly place. I was checking out at the Super 8 Motel one morning and witnessed several children anxiously awaiting a hug from the desk clerk. See if you find that in midtown New York.

This outdoor sports center is a magnet for anglers, hunters, ATV riders, hikers, bikers, canoeists, and snowmobile enthusiasts (average snowfall around here is 50 inches a year). The rush to Park Falls for outdoor adventure is a result of its enviable location at the edge of a vast wilderness and great forests. The town is the headquarters for the Chequamegon National Forest and the unspoiled Turtle Flambeau Flowage.

Park Falls grew up as a lumber town—the first sawmill was built in 1885. By 1890, the area had its first company store, a couple of boardinghouses, and two dozen houses. The lumbering continued on a fast track until the last stand of pine was sawed in 1906. Since then the town has maintained a connection with the forest via the forest products industry. In the center of town you'll see the architecturally interesting Flambeau Paper Company, a building now listed as a historic landmark on the National Register of Historic Places.

Established in 1895, the mill, now operating as the Park Falls Mill of Fraser Papers, is still in full force seven days a week. Other wood-oriented industries in town include Saunders Wood Specialties and Park Falls Hardwoods.

In the center of town is the historic 1895 Park Falls Mill of Fraser Papers.

What else should you know about Park Falls? You'll find out soon upon arrival that this is the Ruffed Grouse Capital of the world. A grouse, often called a partridge, is not often seen because of its excellent camouflage, but you'll know it's a ruffed grouse if you hear a beating sound. Its fast-moving wings emulate the sound of beating drums. The U.S. Forest Service oversees a ruffed grouse habitat of over 5,000 acres in the area.

Events

Annual Butternut Community Fair. Usually the third weekend in August. Billed as "Wisconsin's Biggest Little Fair," this event packs a wallop with farm and garden exhibits, artwork, bingo, horseshoes, and, believe it or not, an animal swap. In the Community Park in Butternut, 6 miles north of Park Falls on WI 13.

Flambeau Rama. The first weekend in August, Thursday through Sunday. One of the oldest celebrations in Wisconsin, this event includes a frog-jumping contest, bed races, bands, arts and crafts, sidewalk sales, and lots more. In the heart of Park Falls in Triangle Park.

Lodging

Many lodges and inns in this area accept pets. Ask about individual requirements when making a reservation.

Ron's Northern Pines Resort and Restaurant. Housekeeping cabins come with linens (except for towels and dishcloths) and a boat. Other features

75

include a dining room, children's playground, and a good fishing lake with two piers. Hunting dogs allowed when brought during hunting season. Four miles northwest of Park Falls on Butternut Lake. N16243 Lakeshore Drive, Butternut. (715) 762-3001.

Unspoiled wilderness woods and waters in the Park Falls area.

Moose Jaw Resort. Lakefront log cabins with screened porches. Trails for hiking, biking, ATVs, and snowmobiles. Sandy beach and playground. Charming lodge dining room features sandwiches, pizza, chicken, fish, and ribs. Open year-round. Pets allowed. Located on the west shore of Round Lake, N15098 Shady Knoll Road, Park Falls. (715) 762-3028.

Northway Motor Lodge. Sauna, hot tub, and spa available. Weekend specials. Pets welcome with permission. WI 13 south of Park Falls. (715) 762-2406 or (800) 844-7144.

Super 8 Motel. One of the newest accommodations in town. Cable TV and free coffee. Pets allowed. About a mile south of the Chequamegon Forest's headquarters at 1212 WI 13, south of Park Falls. (715) 762-3383.

Wild Goose Resort. A snowmobiler's heaven. Fully equipped cottages are located in the midst of the Chequamegon and are at the center of good cross-country and snowmobile trails. Boat rentals, bar, and, yes, pizza. But no pets. Located on Round Lake, part of the Pike Lake chain. N15061 Thoroughfare Road, Park Falls. (800) 884-6673.

Out to Eat

This area loves its pizza. You'll find pizza offered at a wide variety of establishments not usually associated with the Italian pie, such as traditional supper clubs.

Ron's Northern Pines Resort and Restaurant. Country dining in a lodge atmosphere. Dining room has pleasant views of the east shore of Butternut Lake and serves barbecued ribs, deep-fried chicken, pizza, and sandwiches. N16243 Lakeshore Drive, Butternut. (715) 762-3001.

Liebelt's Supper Club. House specials include an 8-ounce filet mignon and savory 16-ounce T-bone steaks. Good pizza too. Other choices include spaghetti and sandwiches. 344 Division Street, Park Falls. (715) 762-3481.

Randy's Family Restaurant. Hearty breakfasts (served anytime), lunch, and dinner. Lasagna, pizza (you're reminded of that fact when you walk in—12-, 14-, and 16-inch pizza pans are displayed by the register), and subs. They make a memorable carrot cake too. WI 13 south of Park Falls. (715) 762-2090.

The Ruffed Grouse Inn. Nice selection of American and German dishes. Many flock here for the huge Bloomin' Onion appetizer—so filling, it's a small meal in itself. And pizza too. WI 13 north of Park Falls. (715) 762-2222.

Wildlife

There are two wildlife refuges in the Park Falls area—the Hoffman Lake-Hay Creek Wildlife Area northeast of town and the Kimberly Clark Wildlife Area southwest of town. Hoffman Lake is a great habitat for the famous ruffed grouse as well as for deer and the black bear. Kimberly Clark has had a hand in tending to the habitat of the sharp-tailed grouse.

The Price County area has long been known as a wildlife refuge for large-antlered deer, ruffed grouse, and black bear. Wherever you are in the area, you're bound to see bald eagles. If you're floating down the Flambeau River, you might see osprey, otter, deer, loons, and fishers. You'll have to go deeper in the forest to see some of the more elusive creatures. Wolves, pine martens, and bobcats all roam the more remote parts of the woods.

Shopping

This is not a shop-till-you-drop sort of place. For example, the downtown area is exceedingly quiet on a Saturday afternoon in midsummer.

Creatively Yours. Many artists and craftspeople contribute to the shop's collection of handmade art, including pottery, jewelry, antiques, and more. 214 Division Street. (715) 762-2064.

Upper Street Apparel. The mix here is men's and women's clothing—many well-known brands like Levis, but just in case you need a tuxedo, you can rent it here as well. 176 S. 3rd Ave. (715) 762-4474.

Chequamegon National Forest

One of the largest national forests in the Midwest is the Chequamegon National Forest. Before European settlers arrived, the Ojibwa Nation lived here for thousands of years. They named the great forest for the "long strip of land and land of shallow waters."

The Chequamegon encompasses 850,000 acres of gently rolling landscape. The statistics associated with its recreational opportunities are staggering. For instance, there are over 365 miles of snowmobile trails, 21 swimming sites, 400 lakes, and 56 developed boat landings. If you want to explore a secluded area, Porcupine Lake and Rainbow Lake Wilderness areas have 11,000 acres of tranquillity that are perfect for hiking. In fact, 52,000 additional acres in the forest have been set aside as semiprivate, nonmotorized areas.

Established in 1933, the forest is home to hundreds of species of wildlife and a wide mix of trees. Many areas have trees that are more than 200 years old. And many of those that were felled in logging operations years ago have been replaced with fast-growing species.

While many wildlife species, like the black bear, have been here for a long time (Glidden calls itself the Black Bear Capital of the world), there are new inhabitants in the Chequamegon. A small population of elk, as well as timber wolves, now inhabit it .

Park Falls is the headquarters of the Chequamegon National Forest. Maps and information are also available at district offices in Medford, Hayward, Washburn, and Glidden.

Sights and Attractions

Smith Rapids Covered Bridge. In 1991, a bridge on the South Fork of the Flambeau River in the Chequamegon needed to be replaced by the U.S. Forest Service. It was thought that the one-lane bridge, which serves U.S. Forest Road 148, would add a unique touch to the wilderness. And it did. (It was also the first covered bridge to be built in Wisconsin in more than 100 years.) The Smith Rapids Bridge is unique not only because it's covered and rises 90 feet above the Flambeau River but also because it is the only glue-laminated, lattice-covered bridge in Wisconsin. At Fifield, go east on WI 70, which gently winds through some of the most beautiful sections of the Chequamegon. After 12 miles, turn left onto Forest Road 148 and go two miles to the bridge.

Round Lake Logging Dam. A few miles east of the covered bridge you'll have a rare opportunity to see a restored logging dam. This dramatic structure was built in 1878 to store logs during the winter months. When the spring thaw opened the river and the log drives began, timber was sluiced through the Round Lake Logging Dam toward distant sawmills. In 1992, the dam was meticulously taken apart in order to restore and reconstruct it. Listed on the National Register of Historic Places, it opened again in 1995. Take WI 70 east of the turnoff for the Smith Rapids Covered Bridge for about eight miles. Turn onto Forest Road 144 at Pike Lake.

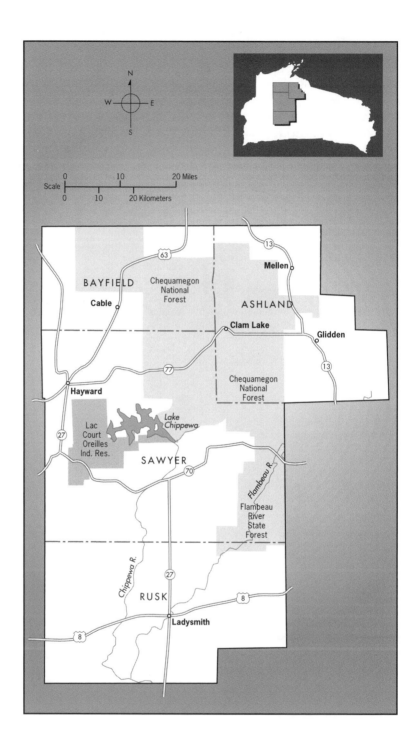

N
W E
S

Scale
0   10   20 Miles
0   10   20 Kilometers

BAYFIELD

63

Chequamegon
National
Forest

Cable

13

Mellen

ASHLAND

Clam Lake

Glidden

77

13

Hayward

Chequamegon
National
Forest

27

Lac
Court
Oreilles
Ind. Res.

Lake
Chippewa

SAWYER

70

Flambeau R.

Flambeau
River
State
Forest

Chippewa R.

27

RUSK

8

Ladysmith

8

chapter 4
the Northwestern Lakes Area

i f you want to get to the heart of the Northwestern Lakes area from the southern reaches of the state as quickly as possible, take I-94 to Eau Claire, then head north on U.S. 53 toward Spooner. Once you're in the Spooner area, turn onto WI 63 and enjoy the 20-mile ride north to Hayward, the region's center of activity and one of Wisconsin's most popular tourist destinations. If you start from Madison and make no stops (next to

impossible for most travelers), the trip will take about five hours. And beyond Hayward, 17 miles to the northeast, you'll find Cable, another spot that attracts outdoor enthusiasts of all kinds. And wait until you see the endless variety of lakes, rivers, forests, and wildlife that surround these two outposts.

Before you get to Hayward, you'll pass miles of rolling hills and tall pine-forested stretches that get you in the mood for outdoor activities. You might be inclined to stop in the unincorporated town of Earl to take a look at the former public-school building, now converted to a two-floor antiques emporium called Schooltime Antiques. Or you might be inspired to stop at the picturesque old white church in Springbrook, now the Springbrook Historical Museum (open only on Fridays in the summer).

Depending on when you arrive in downtown Hayward, it may be hard to believe that the population averages only 2,000 yearround residents. If you're here on a July week-

The Springbrook Historical Museum stands sentry to a wooded clearing off Highway 63.

end, for instance, it may seem as if you and thousands of others have discovered paradise. The annual swell of visitors happens mostly in the summer, but winter also brings an onslaught of visitors because of the world-famous Birkebeiner, the largest cross-country ski event in the United States. The "Birkie" winds its way through Hayward and Cable each February.

For those who love this unique area, with its splendid collection of lakes and rivers, and prime fishing, hunting, skiing, and snowmobile trails, they wouldn't have it any other way. One fan is Wisconsin's governor, Tommy Thompson. You'll see more than one road sign attesting to the fact that the governor has a "northern office" in Hayward.

Big Spider Lake on the Spider Lake Chain, has a picturesque shoreline and many islands.

Barb Grossi, one of the Spider Lake Lodge's owners, in the richly textured North Woods dining room.

First-time visitors to Hayward may be surprised to see a downtown full of fudge shops, moccasin and T-shirt shops, and taverns with stuffed muskies over the bar, not to mention an endless procession of fast-food restaurants. So why else do people come here, you're wondering? To get away from it all. Once you get away from the center of town, you'll find area lakes that have a multitude of family resorts and terrific wilderness areas. In other words, you can be as remote or as urban as you want. If you like bumper-to-bumper traffic, you've got it—if you like un-crowded, pristine wilderness, it's yours. The diversity is what brings the vast number of visitors here every year—to one fantastic forest after another.

If it's a little peace and quiet you're after, then there's no better example than the **Spider Lake Lodge Bed and Breakfast**, 16 miles east of Hayward. When you open the door and cross the threshold into the lobby and great room, you may think of the Robert Redford film *A River Runs through It* and how pristine water and wilderness locations can be the most alluring places on earth. If Hollywood ever makes a film in which a rustic lodge is necessary to capture the essence of Wisconsin's north country, there's no need to look any further than Spider Lake Lodge. This old log lodge is one of the grand old retreats of the northern Wisconsin. Deep, comfortable chairs and couches circle the wall-sized stone fireplace, and everywhere are treetop views of Big Spider Lake, a class-A muskie spot and one link in a five-lake chain.

If its walls could talk, the lodge would have a host of intriguing tales to tell. One of the most interesting pertains to the lodge's beginnings. In 1923, Ted Moody, purported to be one of Al Capone's auto mechanics in Chicago, was encouraged to move north because of his health. He chose the north shore of Spider Lake and took it upon himself to build a boating and fishing resort full of great style and pizzazz.

Around the fireplace at Spider Lake Lodge.

Moody and a crew of lumbermen built the lodge from native logs in the surrounding forest. The monstrous tamarack and cedar beams used to create the lodge still give it a feeling of rustic splendor. Throughout the inside of the lodge, Smith's use of chinking—the art of custom fitting wood pieces between logs by hand—is awe inspiring. According to Barb Grossi, one of the lodge's owners, it took Smith one hour per foot to chink the lodge's interior.

When Ted Moody's Camp, which included the main lodge and 12 cabins, opened as a boating and fishing retreat, the news got around. The lodge attracted large numbers of visitors each summer, many from Moody's old stomping ground in Chicago. If you're curious about those early times, the lodge has plenty of memorabilia to peruse, including an old scrapbook and a muskie-fishing contest registration book in the dining room.

Min and Paul Grossi became the lodge's third owners when they bought it in 1973. In 1990, the Grossi family thought that the lodge was in need of serious restoration after over 70 years in operation. They decided to transform it into a bed and breakfast. The adjacent cabins were sold, and the Grossis concentrated on restoring and updating the lodge so guests could enjoy its special warmth. Before the restoration, there were no bedrooms in the main lodge and only 2 bathrooms. Now there are 7 bedrooms and 11 bathrooms. The public rooms, such as the dining room and great room, have been painstakingly preserved in keeping with the character of the original building. After restoration, the lodge added "Bed and Breakfast" to its name. (Min and her daughter-in-law, Barb, now own and run the lodge together.) The spellbinding beauty of the area, combined with the charm of the historic lodge above the water, are the same reasons vacationers were first drawn here over 75 years ago.

Historic landmark church east of Hayward at the intersection of Highway 77 and Murphy Boulevard.

Hayward

Hayward, the seat of Sawyer County, became a gateway to the area and a popular commercial spot when the region became a big timber producer in the late 1880s. By 1880 the town also had a name. A. J. Hayward, a well-heeled lumberman, bought a sawmill on the Namekagon River, then founded the

North Western Lumber Company. Subsequently, Hayward wrap-ped its sig-nificance around his name. As the lumber industry mushroomed, the town made a name for itself as a raucous and wild boomtown, rivaling Hurley to the north. It seems that lumbermen with little extra change in their pockets chose Hayward as the place to spend it all in one night.

Raised wooden trail at Copper Falls State Park.

Hayward has calmed down considerably since then, but it's retained its commercial flavor. Now, what you'll see in the middle of town are vast num-bers of convenience stores and fast-food restaurants. No excuse in Hayward to run out of gas, fudge, or ice cream.

Drive into town and you'll be enticed into spending time in a variety of entertainment spots. There's the Hayward Amusement Park on WI 27; Fiddlers Creek Driving Range, south of town on U.S. 63, offers par-three golf and minature golf; and Windmill Square on Highway 27 south of town, where the cottage of Lynn Marie's Candies draws them in. Shopping for candy, after all, is a northern Wisconsin tradition. Another place for good fudge is Tremblay's Sweet Shop, downtown on Main Street, across from the Tru-Value Hardware store.

Once you get to downtown Hayward, at the corner of WI 27 and U.S. 63, it's hard to resist the Moccasin Bar—the sign outside says that it's the home of the world's biggest muskie. And who's going to argue with that boast once you go in and take a gander? This stuffed beauty is five-feet long and worth the look. The tavern draws the curious but it's also a good place to absorb the Hayward scene.

Now that you've found your way to downtown Hayward, get outside and enjoy the splendid rivers, lakes, and forests all around you. After all, that's what most visitors come here for. The area offers over 600 miles of groomed snowmobile trails, superb golf courses, groomed cross-country and snowmobile trails through tall stands of pine—all that, plus the awesome beauty of the area's forests and lakes. **For more information, contact the Hayward Area Chamber of Commerce. (715) 634-8662.**

Hayward's National Fresh Water Fishing Hall of Fame.

Sights and Attractions

The Hideout. What is it about gangsters? Their offbeat lifestyle seems to bring out an overwhelming curiosity in all of us. Here, at Capone's early-1920s compound in Couderay, 17 miles southeast of Hayward, the curious have a lot to fascinate them. For starters, the 500-acre retreat, built on a hill in a scenic lakeside setting, takes you back to the days when the thugs were in luxurious hiding. The property now houses a museum full of interesting memorabilia. You can also see a recreation of the famous 1929 St. Valentine's Day Massacre. Take the tour and you'll pass by the gun tower where Capone's sentries kept watch over the property. For many, the most intriguing part of the visit is a chance to take in Capone's old stone lodge and its beautifully constructed fireplace and dramatic staircase. No need to rush off, the dining room features everything from Chicago-style (naturally) sandwiches to chicken and steaks. In fact, many savvy travelers know this as place for good food, period. Never mind that it's also filled with history. Take WI 27south and east to Couderay, then go north 6 miles on County CC. 12101W County CC. (715) 945-2746.

Louie Baron the Voyageur. If you've always wondered what it was like to paddle an authentic birchbark canoe, here's your chance. Louie Baron the Voyageur, with you and others as crew, will paddle along in a fully restored 36-foot canoe from the fur-trading days. During your outing Louie brings history alive by sharing stories and songs of the days of LaSalle, the great adventurer. Voyages depart in summer, one mile south of Hayward on Highway B. For reservations contact Spirit of the Voyageur. (715) 634-7651.

National Fresh Water Fishing Hall of Fame. There's no way to miss the massive muskie outside, probably the biggest one in the universe. This walk-through wonder is 143-feet tall-that's 4.5 stories. You'll see visitors walking around its observation deck (in the form of a giant mouth), gazing at the Hayward area below. (Dozens of weddings have been performed in the creature's mouth.) But don't let that theme-park look fool you. This is a serious historical museum. The four buildings showcase a huge variety of rods and reels, over 400 mounted fish, 350 outboard motors, and a whole lot more. Fishing aficionados shouldn't miss it. Open mid-April through November 1. Hall of Fame Drive, just off WI 27, in downtown Hayward. (715) 634-4440.

Scheer's Lumberjack Shows. Every brave feat you'd expect from burly lumberjacks: chopping, canoe jousting, pole climbing, ax throwing, logrolling, and more. Rain or shine, you'll see

Poison Ivy

In Wisconsin's woods are filled with wondrous scenic beauty. Those who enjoy the outdoors should also be cognizant of the fact that these same scenic forests are also home to the bountiful poison ivy plant. You may think that all poison ivy has a certain number of leaves, such as the well-known three-leaf variety. Actually, poison ivy cloaks itself in a variety of ways, so identification can be tricky. Remember that poison ivy leaves cluster in odd numbers only; in addition to the three-numbered variety, they also grow as five-, seven-, and even nine-leafed plants. Learn to identify the basic plant, then be careful if you see leaves clustered in more numbers than you'd expect.

What can you do to combat the itching from the poison ivy rash? If you think you've come in contact with poison ivy and you're still near the plant, look for jewelweed growing in the same area. This plant has soft orange blossoms, grows close to poison ivy, and, oddly enough, offers a quick cure. Take a jewelweed leaf and rub it over the rash or drip juice from its leaves onto the irritated area. Catnip is another natural remedy. All you have to do is squeeze juice from its leaves and you should feel a soothing effect right away.

Remember, you can still get a poison ivy rash from dead or dried poison ivy. But the rash cannot be transmitted from one person to another. The only way you can get poison ivy is by touching the oil on the plant.

what you came for since performances are held in a covered grandstand, also known as the "holding area" for logs back in the 1890s. Showtimes: Tuesday,

Thursday, and Saturday at 7:30 P.M.; matinees Tuesday, Wednesday, Thursday, and Saturday at 2:00 P.M. Located one mile south of Hayward on County B at the Lumberjack Village Pancake House, across the street from the Sawyer County Historical Museum. (715) 634-5010.

Wilderness Walk. This is a great place to bring the family, see animals up close and personal, and get some exercise. There is a wide variety of animals for viewing, from arctic foxes to otters. Your walk begins with a view of baby animals in the nursery, then proceeds to tame deer, farm animals, and many others like badgers and beavers. A creek running through the 35-acre property offers gold panning, picnicking, and duck watching. Open daily mid-May through Labor Day. Three miles south of Hayward on WI 27. (715) 634-2893.

Wildlife Museum and Bar. Since we're talking muskies, if you haven't gotten your fill at the Fresh Water Hall of Fame, then the Wildlife Museum and Bar is a must-see. This interesting spot has 68 mounted muskies, a world record. But that's not all. There are also more than 600 animal mounts, including polar bears and cougars. The artist who painted the scenes for the famed Milwaukee Natural History Museum has painted the background motifs depicting the animals in their wild habitat. Once you've toured the museum, a friendly bar staff offers up your favorite drink in a pub that includes pool, darts, and other games. Open daily, year-round. Small admission fee for the museum. Located at the intersection of County B and Hall of Fame Drive. (715) 634-3386.

Events

Lumberjack World Championships. The third weekend of July is when the world's best lumberjacks congregate in Hayward to compete in every form of wood-cutting and log-rolling event imaginable. Covered by national TV, the three-day event goes runs from 9 A.M. to 5 P.M. The professional competition usually starts in the early afternoon. Other features include demonstrations, exhibits, and music. (715) 634-2484.

Musky Festival. A few downtown streets are roped off for this annual four-day festival in mid-June. Highlights include the Musky Festival Parade, ice cream and watermelon eating contests, prize drawings, arts and crafts, sidewalk sales, lumberjack shows, and fishing on local lakes. (715) 634-8662.

Lodging

There are so many different types of accommodations in the Hayward area, it's unlikely that you could ever arrive here and not find a room, even without a reservation. The area is saturated with endless accommodations, including inns, upscale resorts, vacation homes, down-home cottages, bed and breakfasts, cabins, lodges, and motels. At last count, there were approximately 135 lodging facilities in the area. Check with the Hayward Area Chamber of Commerce, (715) 634-8662; or the Hayward Lakes Resort Association, (715) 634-4801.

Chief Lake Lodge. Housekeeping cottages have scenic locations on the Chippewa Flowage. Popular Friday night fish fry, full breakfasts, pizza, and snacks are on the menu in the main lodge. Pontoon and paddleboat rental. Bait and fishing tackle available. Open year-round, seven days a week. Hayward. (715) 945-2221.

The Lumberman's Mansion. Jan Hinrichs Blaedel and Wendy Hinrichs Sanders run this carefully restored 1887 mansion. The elegant five-bedroom home, now an inviting bed and breakfast (full breakfasts each morning), is brimming with period antiques. Warm, friendly atmosphere. City convenience, country calm. 15844 E. 4th Street. Hayward. (715) 634-3012.

Northland Lodge. Completely furnished log vacation homes on quiet Lost Land Lake. In 1921, log cabins were built on this outstanding lakefront property where a logging camp once thrived. The main lodge has a game room and cocktail lounge. Paddleboats, canoes, kayaks, and sailboats are available for rental. The third generation of the Thearin family manages this wonderful old establishment. Open year-round. Ask about the special spring/fall fishing packages. Hayward. (715) 462-3379.

Ross's Teal Lake Lodge. Classic log lodge built in 1907

ELK

Native elk haven't roamed Wisconsin's woods since the 1850s, but now all that has changed. In 1995 Ray Anderson, retired professor of wildlife at the University of Wisconsin-Stevens Point, headed an independent group interested in reintroducing elk into the Chequamegon National Forest. That year, 25 elk from a herd in Minnesota were shipped to an area about four miles south of Clam Lake. Once this private venture got off the ground, the Department of Natural Resources, the U.S. Forest Service, the University of Wisconsin-Stevens Point, and the Rocky Mountain Elk Foundation joined forces to help reestablish elk herds in the state. In 1998, there were approximately 50 elk in the same Clam Lake area. The results of a four-year study of the elk will be evaluated, with the final decision about their future resting with the State of Wisconsin.

Elk become alarmed if you get too close, so stay your distance. When elk become frightened and run from danger, the resulting stress burns up their body fat, which they critically need for surviving long winters. If you come upon an elk, it may signal you're too close by assuming an "alarmed" look. Its posture becomes erect and rigid, making the animal move stiffly. It also might make a sharp "bark," warning other elk you're in the area.

Different characteristics of elk and white-tailed deer:
* Antlers curve forward on deer, backward on elk.
* Tails of deer are long with white coloring on the underside, while elk's tails are very small.
* Deer are about three feet at the shoulders, elk stand between four and five feet at the shoulders.

retains an old fishing camp at-mosphere. The lodge, surrounded by cabins and townhouselike suites, is a nostalgic retreat located on Teal Lake. Teal has a 10-mile-an-hour speed limit for boats and jet-skis, so you don't hear a lot of noise from jet-skis or boats. This 220-acre resort, offering flexible American-plan meals, has been in the Ross family for over 75 years. As a result, some things never change, which is what repeat guests count on—like the bountiful chicken dinner served every Sunday night in the dining room since the lodge opened. The Ross family has added the Teal Wing Golf Club—championship tees play 6,500 yards, the foremost tees play 3,800 yards. Twenty miles east of Hayward on WI 77. (715) 462-3631.

Spider Lake Lodge Bed and Breakfast. See the introduction to this chapter for a description of its many charms. I must add here that the rotating breakfasts are fabulous and are often embellished with fresh flowers. There are seven guest rooms in the lodge overlooking Big Spider Lake. Sixteen miles east of Hayward, off WI 77. (715) 462-3793 or 800-OLD WISC.

Out to Eat

Club 77. This is a favorite local dining spot. The club, appropriately named since it's right on Highway 77, features everything you'd expect from a supper club, including burgers, steak, and seafood. One specialty that's put it on the map is the succulent roast duck with wild rice. Superb Black Angus rib-eyes, porterhouse and New York strip steaks, filet mignon, and top sirloin. Serving starts at 5:00 P.M. seven days a week from early June to October 1. Closed on Tuesdays and Wednesdays from October through mid-March, and closed completely from late-March through early April. About seven miles east of Hayward on WI 77. (715) 462-3712.

Famous Dave's BBQ Shack. Don't let the name fool you. This isn't a shack. Instead, it's a rustic log gathering spot on the shore of Big Round Lake. Tired of supper club fare? Then Dave Anderson at Famous Dave's has just the thing—slow-cooked, hickory-smoked, barbecued ribs, beef, and chicken. The down-home cooking also includes corn muffins and coleslaw—all presented in a rustic atmosphere. Before you leave (or stay awhile and rent one of the adjacent cabins) visit the gift shop and take home some of Dave's famous barbecue sauce. Open year-round. Eight and half miles east of Hayward on County B. (715) 462-3352.

Flat Creek Eatery and Saloon. If you ask one of the locals where to find good food, chances are they'll steer you here. Large menu choices include great burgers, imaginative salads, hand-tossed pizza, steak, shrimp, and sinfully rich desserts. Odd and wildly different house specials include the popular cinnamon chicken. Located in Country Inns and Suites. One mile south of downtown Hayward on WI 27. (715) 634-1466.

Karibalis. A downtown Hayward institution for more than 75 years, "Karb's" offers many favorite choices, ranging from sandwiches to fancy dinners. Sandwich specialties include their irresistible burgers (modesty aside, they'll tell you they make the world's best burgers), brats, and Reubens. Hungry for something in between sandwiches and steaks? No problem. They've got plenty of choices like burritos, Cajun chicken, and stir-fry chicken. Sit in front of the fireplace and enjoy one of their famous steak Diane dinners, jumbo battered shrimp, or prime rib on Saturday nights. This busy, popular spot has a kids' menu, free balloons for the taking, and deck for outdoor sprawling. 212 Main Street. (715) 634-2462.

Tally-Ho. The restaurant has been going strong since 1944 when ice was put up for the year from nearby Spider Lake. Why are northern Wisconsin supper clubs so dark that it takes a moment for your eyes to get used to the interior light (or absence of it)? Someone long ago probably figured the dimmer the lights, the cozier the atmosphere. Sometimes the theory works, sometimes it doesn't. At Tally-Ho it adds to the cozy hunt-room atmosphere. As the name implies, this spot has an English countryside theme. Pictures of English hunt scenes line the dining-room walls, while a piano player handles the background music in the adjacent bar. The bread and relish tray are so large, they resemble an entree. Specialties include veal marsala, slow-roasted prime rib, and sirloin steak. Try the tenderloin kabob—a winner. About 15 miles east of Hayward on WI 77. Reservations preferred, especially for Saturday nights in the summer. (715) 462-3646.

Lightning Tips

Chances are that lightning won't strike anywhere near you when you're engaged in outdoor activities. Estimates by the National Weather Service report that 100 people are killed by lightning each year and another 300 people are injured. These are fairly small numbers, yet they represent the largest number of deaths caused by weather in the United States. Since most north country visitors spend a lot of time outdoors, it's a good idea to review these lightning tips with your family.

* If you're in a car and can't get to shelter, make sure your car's windows are securely rolled up. If you're outdoors in a thunderstorm:
* Crouch in a gulley or the lowest area around you;
* Don't huddle with a group—keep your distance from other people;
* Immediately get out of the water if you're swimming or boating;
* Avoid metal objects like wire fences, railings, and clothes lines;
* Avoid being on or near metal objects like bikes and golf carts.

Cable

Cable, located in Bayfield County, is in the middle of a four-season recreation area, but autumn is when it really sparkles as those who know where to find splashy fall color end up here. The small town, 17 miles northeast of Hayward on U.S. 63, is popular as a gateway for hiking, biking, and exploring the Chequamegon National Forest.

Cable is proud of the fact that it has been designated as one of 30 "Trail Towns" around the country. That means that there are over 300 mapped trails for mountain-bike riders in the area. The route runs from Hayward to Iron River and was created by the Chequamegon Area Mountain Bike Association (CAMBA). Even though Cable is tiny, the area around it, which includes Lake Owen and Lake Namekagon, has a vast array of lodges, resorts, cabins, and other accommodations. One of the more unusual is **Garmisch USA**, a lodge and assemblage of housekeeping facilities that resemble an estate in the Bavarian Alps. The great room of the main lodge has magnificent floor-to-ceiling windows for enjoying the views. You'll never get cold here—there are 21 fireplaces in the main "castle." It's located on Lake Namekagon, 10 miles east of Cable. (715) 794-2204 or (800) 794-2204.

A well-known Cable landmark is the **Telemark Resort**, located three miles east of town. This large, chaletlike year-round resort was permanently closed in early 1999 but is sure to reopen under new management before too long.

Since 1907, the **Lakewoods Resort and Forest Ridges Golf Course** has been drawing families to its scenic spot in the Chequamegon National Forest, between the Rock Lake Primitive Area and Lake Namekagon. The resort is now in its fourth generation of family ownership. Extensive year-round amenities include indoor and outdoor swimming pools, an 18-hole golf course, driving range, horseback riding, fishing, marina, snowmobiling, cross-country skiing, and more. This is one of the country's premier snowmobile resorts. Eight miles east of Cable on Lake Namekagon. (715) 794-2561 or (800) 255-5937.

For more information, call the Cable Area Visitor Center, (715) 798-3833 or (800) 533-7454. Or visit the center on County M, one block east of U.S. 63.

Sights and Attractions

Cable Natural History Museum. If you want to know more about this area, you won't have to go far out of your way. This well-organized museum offers lots of behind-the-scenes information. You'll learn how to identify trees, wildlife, insects, and birds of the area. This is a good place for children and parents to get a head start on having a memorable vacation. For more in-depth education, query the museum's naturalist. Open year-round, Tuesday through Sunday. Located on M, two blocks east of U.S. 63.

Events

Chequamegon Fat Tire Festival. This annual biking event has been increasing in popularity each year since its inception in 1983. The Trek corporation has been a major sponsor since 1993. It is so popular that in 1997, for example, the maximum number of registrations, 2,500, sold out in 24 hours. As a result, the organizers have had to change registration procedures. Armies of bikers descend upon the area the third weekend of September for this world-class event in the Chequamegon National Forest. Downtown Hayward celebrates with bicycle parades and a lot of hoopla. Kids decorate their bikes for a bicycle parade before the big events. For more information, call (715) 798-3594.

The DYNO American Birkebeiner Ski Race. The Birkie, the largest cross-country ski race in America, originated in Hayward in 1973. If you've ever seen the IMAX version of the ski race on a big movie screen, you can appreciate the pounding adrenaline as nearly 8,000 skiers whip across snow-packed terrain. Fifty-three area ski enthusiasts began it all by racing from Hayward to Cable's Telemark Resort. Their challenge was to emulate the great Norwegian Birkebeiner. The American version has become so popular that skiers from Norway have become one of the largest group of contenders. In fact, skiers descend upon Hayward and Cable from all over the world. The three-day event in mid-February features many spin-off celebrations, such as fun races, snowmobile races, speed races, torchlight races, and children's races.

Lodging

See the "Lodging" section under Hayward for nearby accommodations.

Lac Courte Oreilles Indian Reservation

The Lac Courte Oreilles (means "lake of short ears") Indian Reservation encompasses 31,000 acres southeast of Hayward. This is home base to the Lac Courte Oreilles Band of Lake Superior Chippewa. The reservation is located in the enviable position of being next to the Chequamegon National Forest and the Chippewa Flowage.

The Lac Courte Oreilles Casino features slot machines and blackjack tables. The casino's restaurant, the Wigwam Buffet and Restaurant, presents a 21-item salad bar and popular all-you-can-eat buffets. Lunch and dinner buffets are served seven days a week. The restaurant also offers a variety of daily menu selections. The lodge has a cozy great room surrounding a fieldstone fireplace, a convention center, and, in the indoor-pool room, yes, another fireplace to add to the rustic ambiance. Nearby, good snowmobile trails are ready and waiting. Four miles east of Hayward on County B. Casino and restaurant. (800) 526-2274; lodge, (800) 526-5634.

Event

Honor The Earth Powwow. This annual event began as a peaceful protest after the 1923 flooding of Ojibwa land by the National States Power Company to create the Chippewa Flowage. The festive commemoration features ceremonies, games, dancing, sports, and food. Many tribes and nations traditionally participate. The public is welcome at the Lac Courte Oreilles tribal grounds. Eleven miles southeast of Hayward, at the junction of County K and County E. Tribal Office, (715) 634-8934.

Lake Chippewa Flowage

If you like scenic lake islands and lots of water, you'll love it here. Lake Chippewa Flowage is the state's third largest lake and its largest wilderness lake. It all started in 1923 when the Northern States Power Company put a dam across the Chippewa River. After 11 lakes and 9 rivers overflowed, the water emptied into what became the Chippewa Flowage. The result? More than 17,000 acres of water and 140 islands.

Get out on the "Big Chip," as it's affectionately known, and you're apt to see bald eagles, blue herons, beavers, and white-tailed deer feeding on shore. The best time to visit the "Big Chip"? For many, it's in the fall when the power company boosts power by lowering the lake 12 feet. The lowered lake offers a chance to gaze at sand and rock formations previously visible by fish eyes only. The Chippewa Queen Tours operates the *Denum Lacey*, a 40-foot-long, glass-enclosed touring boat for restful cruises on the flowage. This is a good way to view wildlife and learn about the culture and history of the area's first residents. Oscar Treland, who knows the area better than just about anyone else around, adds a personal touch to his narration. A variety of cruises are offered including two- and three-hour dinner cruises. The *Denum Lacey* accommodates up to 50 passengers for general cruising, 34 for dinner cruises. It docks at **Treeland Resorts** (see below).

Event

Fishing Has No Boundaries. This three-day event in mid-May is the first fishing festival for disabled people in the world, originating in Hayward in 1988. It annually attracts disabled anglers of all ages, from far and wide. Located on the Chippewa Flowage at the Lake Chippewa Campground. To register, call (715) 634-3185.

Lodging

Treeland Resorts. The property has been in the Treland family since Oluf Treland ventured here from Norway and set down stakes. Oluf's son, Oscar, took over in 1963. The resort features furnished vacation homes, motel suites, a heated outdoor pool, tennis courts, kayaks, paddleboats, canoes. water-skiing, and well-manicured snowmobile and cross-country trails right outside the door. The resort's full restaurant offers a continental menu including outstanding prime rib on Saturday nights. On the Chippewa Flowage, about 15 miles east of Hayward on County B. (715) 462-3874.

Clam Lake and Glidden

Set on the far western edge of Ashland County, at the intersection of WI

77, County M, and County GG, the town of Clam Lake enjoys a matchless position in the heart of the Chequamegon National Forest. Plenty of lakes, streams, and campgrounds in the area make it easy to enjoy the great outdoors. In the town itself, there are a few retail establishments, such as gas stations and a grocery store, but visitors to this neck of the woods don't come here to be coddled by comfortable surroundings. There's one exception though. That's **Clam Lake Lodge**, the only inn and restaurant on Clam Lake. Locals will tell you it's one of the best lunch and dinner spots in all of northwest Wisconsin. Recently renovated, the lodge features five bedrooms and a separate cabin with a complete kitchen. This is where locals go to celebrate a special occasion. More than a lodge, more than a restaurant, this is a place with culinary treasures and a picturesque setting that will have you hooked. The restaurant, serves lunch and dinner from 11:30 A.M. to 9 P.M. Closed Tuesdays. (715) 794-2518.

The unincorporated town of Glidden, in southern Ashland County, has plenty of small cafes, like the popular Red Rooster Cafe, where you can stop and ponder the fact that you've arrived in the Black Bear Capital of Wisconsin. Evidence of this is that during the 1963 bear hunting season, a hunter brought down a black bear that stood more than 10 and a half feet and weighed 665 pounds. Glidden has many picturesque recreational areas, like Marian Park, a historical treasure with its wonderfully old eight-sided pavilion. And lest you forget the town's legacy, signs pointing the way around Glidden are adorned with, you guessed it, fierce-looking bears.

The Natural Scenic Byway, which runs from Glidden to Clam Lake through the Chequamegon National Forest, offers splendid scenery. A good time to visit is in the fall, when the surrounding forests, the Chequamegon and Nicolet are at their showiest. If you come by during Labor Day weekend, expect to find a well-attended community fair, complete with arts and crafts, music, and festivities. **Call the Glidden Area Chamber of Commerce, (715) 264-4304.**

Mellen

The small town of Mellen, population 1,000, oozes charm. It's known primarily as the gateway to the majestic Copper Falls State Park, just north of town. Located on hilly terrain next to the Penokee Mountain Range, Mellen still sports an old-fashioned Victorian look. Several homes and commercial buildings have been nicely restored. One of these is the white clapboard 1896 Mellen City Hall, which is listed on the National Register of Historic Places. As you're driving north through town, you'll pass this structure on your right. Currently, the building houses the Mellen Library, Mellen Historical Museum, and city government offices. Another reason to stop and unwind at Mellen is the fine nine-hole Mellen Country Club, which is open to the public; it has several promotions during the week, such as "ladies day" on Tuesdays and "men's day" on Wednesdays. Just north of town, off U.S. 13 on

The small town of Mellen has many restored historic buildings, including the 1896 City Hall.

County C. (715) 274-7311. **For more information on the Mellen area, contact the Mellen Area Chamber of Commerce. (715) 274-2330.**

Sights and Attractions

Copper Falls State Park. About four miles east of Mellen, you'll see signs leading to Copper Falls State Park. Millions of years ago the Bad River, which originates in east-central Ashland County, began cascading across rock outgrowth in the Mellen area. The result is the wondrous Copper Falls State Park (the falls of the same name has a 29-foot drop), with walled canyons and downstream, Tyler Forks Cascades, and Brownstone Falls.

As you get close to the park, you'll pass Loon Lake on your left, then come to the park entrance. The state park office is located in a new log building, constructed in 1997, where you can pick up plenty of maps and information about the park.

Many visitors come to see the falls, but some don't want to walk far to see them. If that describes you, you're in luck. After you've paid your entrance fee, drive to the parking lot nearest the concession stand and picnic area. Just beyond, you'll see a footbridge crossing the Bad River. If you hike for less than a mile, you'll see some of the park's spectacular falls. By the way, the self-guided trail is far above the gorges below, making for magnificent views. For those who want to spend several hours exploring the sights, the park's trails offer breathtaking vistas around the hiking loop. The park has four hiking trails, including a self-guided section covering seven miles.

There are two camping areas in the park with 56 individual campsites. Swimmers can stake out a spot at the sandy beach on Loon Lake, cross-country skiers have six trail loops to choose from, and anglers can fish the Bad and Tyler Forks Rivers for brown, rainbow, and brook trout.

St. Peter's Dome and Morgan Falls. About 25 miles west of Mellen, you'll find St. Peter's Dome, which rewards those who make the steep, two-hour, one-mile climb with magnificent views of Lake Superior (on clear days) and the splendid Penokee mountain range. At an elevation of approximately 1,600 feet, this is the second highest point in Wisconsin. Morgan Falls, named after a Civil War silver miner, is not difficult to get to. Locals will tell you this is one of their favorite places for hiking and enjoying the outdoors. If you come in winter, expect to be dazzled by dramatic views of the falls as they cascade over rare black rock called black gabbro, also known as black granite. The only other place black gabbro is known to exist is in the Swiss Alps.

Copper Falls State Park.

Take U.S. 13 north of Mellen for about 10 miles to the third exit for County C (if you exit at the first exit for C, at the Mellen Country Club, you'll travel for several miles on unpaved road, only to discover that the road runs back into 13.) At the third C exit, go west for about two miles. Look for FR 187 and turn left. Travel on 187 for about four miles, then turn right on FR 199 and follow it for approximately five miles until you reach the parking lot. The hike to the falls is about one half mile. Follow the sounds of rushing water. If you're going on to the dome, you'll pass the area of the falls, then encounter a steep trek to the summit. **Contact the Glidden Ranger District. (715) 264-2511.**

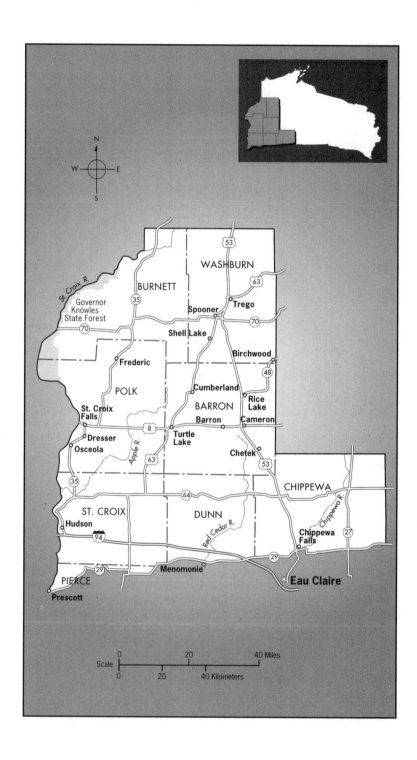

chapter 5
the St. Croix River Valley and Indian Head Country

Eau Claire, Chippewa Falls, and Menomonie

Once the Treaty of 1837 was signed between the United States and the Chippewa (Ojibwa), the Chippewa Valley was officially opened up for lumbering. Over the next 150 years, billions of board feet of lumber were produced in this area. The Chippewa River was a natural highway for getting most of this timber to market. The area's lumber facts speak for themselves: Chippewa Falls had the largest sawmill in the area; the huge lumber producer Knapp, Stout and Company dominated Menomonie's presence; and in the early 1870s, Eau Claire had 11 sawmills.

The area drew thousands of settlers looking for a chance to make a fortune in lumbering. Some did, many others didn't. Droves of immigrant Irish, Norwegians, Germans, and Canadians moved into the area because it reminded them of home. They helped shape the culture and traditions of the Chippewa Valley as it is known today.

Eau Claire (French for "clear water") is located at the intersection of the Eau Claire and Chippewa Rivers. Although it is not always thought of as a northern Wisconsin destination, it's on the the fringe of the region, is the biggest city in this part of the state, and is a good stopping place for travelers venturng farther north. In addition, the city has fine restaurants and museums and many well-groomed parks for leisure activities. If you're going farther north, Eau Claire and the nearby towns of Chippewa Falls and Menomonie are good places for taking time to absorb the abundant historical ambiance and contemporary charm. All three communities, in the midst of rambling hills and splendid river valleys, have numerous historical homes and cultural legacies waiting to be explored. **For more information on the area, contact: (1) the Chippewa Valley Convention and Visitors Bureau, 3625 Gateway Drive, Goft Rd. and U.S. 53, (800) 344-FUNN or (715) 831-2345; (2) the Chippewa Falls Chamber of Commerce, 811 N.**

Bridge Street, (715) 723-0331; (3) the Greater Menomonie Area Chamber of Commerce, 700 Wolske Bay Road, (715) 235-9087.

Sights and Attractions

Augusta. Eighteen miles southeast of Eau Claire lies the attractive one-block-long town of Augusta, home to over 100 Amish families who do without phones, electricity, cars, and other modern conveniences. If you're in the area the first weekend in August, look for the Amish Quilt and Furniture shop at The Woodshed, a retail store in the heart of town. Phone the Chippewa Valley Convention and Visitors Bureau. (715) 831-2345.

Chippewa Valley Museum. Known as one of the finest regional historical museums in Wisconsin, it houses exhibits tracing the history of the Ojibwa. You'll also see a 21-room dollhouse, a 1-room schoolhouse, an old-fashioned ice cream parlor still operating, and a Scandinavian-designed log home. Located in lovely Carson Park, Eau Claire's premier playground, the museum is open year-round, Tuesday through Sunday. Take I-94 or U.S. 53 to West Clairemont Avenue, to Menomonie Street, then east to Carson Park Drive. Admission is free. (715) 834-7871.

Chippewa Valley Railroad Association. Train rides over one half mile of narrow-gauge tracks pulled by authentic steam locomotives. Train buffs should visit the depot, roundhouse and check out the oldest interlocking signal tower in Wisconsin. Open Memorial Day through Labor Day. Carson Park. (715) 835-7500.

Fanny Hill Inn and Dinner Theater. A dinner theater with a difference, not the least of which is the beautiful Victorian inn that's part of the entire operation (see "Lodging" below). Its views of the dramatic Chippewa Valley are glorious and the food is more than passable, which is often not the case with dinner theaters. Fanny Hill's fare is truly memorable; plus, the shows are more than worth the price of admission. Open Thursday through Sunday, matinees Wednesday, Thursday, and Friday. Three miles southwest of Eau Claire at 3919 Crescent Avenue (County EE). (715) 836-8186.

Lake Wissota State Park. A good spot for cross-country skiing on more than seven miles of groomed trails. You won't get bored on this ever-changing terrain. Daily park fee or annual state park pass. Take WI 178 north out of Chippewa Falls, then right on County S, then right on County O. (715) 382-4574.

The Leinie Lodge Gift Shop and Jacob Leinenkugel Brewing Company. When Jacob Leinenkugel came to Wisconsin in 1867 he was looking for the perfect place to brew beer. He found what he was looking for in Chippewa Falls—plentiful spring water, barley, and hops. Thousands stop here every year to take a tour of this venerable Wisconsin institution. Advance tour reservations suggested. One Jefferson Avenue, WI 124, Chippewa Falls. (715) 723-5557.

Mabel Tainter Memorial Theater. This splendid 1890 Victorian theater was named for a young woman passionate about the arts who died at the age of 19. The theater's opulent interior, often called one of America's most magnificent examples of Victorian decor, is resplendent with colorful leaded-glass windows, a marble staircase, and lavish fireplaces. Visitors can browse the art gallery, reading room, and gift shop. Daily tours of the theater year-round. 205 Main Street, Menomonie. (800) 236-7675 or (715) 235-0001.

Paul Bunyan Logging Camp. Carson Park is also home to this actual 1890s logging camp. Everything you've always wanted to know about living in a logging camp is here, along with a bunkhouse, blacksmith shop, cook-shack, barn, and more. Open from mid-April through Labor Day. Admission is free. (715) 835-6200.

Events

Country Fest. Twenty miles east of Eau Claire, on the grounds of the Chippewa Valley Music Festival in Cadott, you'll find musical frenzy at its finest. It's not unusual for over 100,000 fans to gather here to see top draws like Vince Gill and Mary Chapin Carpenter. Festival seating, 7,000 campsites, food vendors, a huge screen for close-up action, and closed-circuit TVs. Who could ask for more? The two-day festival is held at the end of June. (800) 326-FEST.

Country Jam USA. The largest country jamboree in the state takes place over four days during the third week in July. Top talent such as LeAnn Rimes, Wynona, and Alabama regularly perform. One of the largest outdoor country music festivals anywhere in the U.S. Food aplenty on these grounds on the west side of Eau Claire, on the shores of the Chippewa River. Go southwest on Crescent Avenue (County EE) and look for the signs.

Festival in the Pines. This festival brings together more than 250 artists and craftspeople who exhibit their wares in a lively environment replete with storytellers, jugglers, and musicians. Carson Park. Mid-August. (715) 834-7337 or (888) 611-7463.

International Fall Festival. If you never get a chance to travel outside the United States, here's your chance to sample culture and food from other countries, as downtown Eau Claire brims with international food vendors, folk art, and entertainment. And no international celebration in Wisconsin would be complete without a German beer garden. There's that and a lot more. Two days in mid-September. (800) 344-FUNN.

Winterfest. A mighty winter celebration worth a special trip. Sleigh rides, heated fun tent, snow slide, and lots more. Held over five days in mid-January. Carson Park. (800) 344-FUNN.

Lodging
CHIPPEWA FALLS

Pleasant View Bed and Breakfast. On the shores of Lake Wissota, four enchanting guest rooms complete with whirlpool, bath, and queen-size bed. Woods and water right outside the door. 16649 96th Avenue. (715) 382-4401.
MENOMONIE

Bolo Country Inn. Twenty-five guest rooms exuding country ambiance.

101

Restaurant on premises, where you have to try the popular light-as-air popovers. 207 Pine Avenue. (715) 235-5596.

EAU CLAIRE

Antlers. A tidy motel that features cable TV and complimentary coffee, tea, and pastries. 2245 Hastings Way, at U.S. 12 and 53. (800) 423-4526 or (715) 834-5313.

AMERICINN Motel and Suites. Amenities include an indoor pool, whirlpool, and sauna. Some suites have in-room whirlpools and fireplaces. Complimentary continental breakfast. 6200 Texaco Drive. Take Exit 59 off I-94. (800) 634-3444.

Fanny Hill Inn. In the same location as the dinner theater mentioned in "Sights and Attractions" on page 100. Romantic spot with Victorian gardens. The 11 guest rooms feature whirlpools and complimentary continental breakfast. On-site restaurant. 3919 Crescent Avenue. (800) 292-8026 or (715) 836-8184.

Hampton Inn. Nicely furnished inn oriented to families. Indoor pool, whirlpool, and exercise room. Complimentary continental breakfast. Kids under 18 stay free when accompanied by parents. 2622 Craig Road. Off I-94, take WI 37 north to Exit 65. (800) HAMPTON or (715) 833-0003.

Maple Manor Motel. The attractive decor reflects the area's woods and nature. Free breakfast in the adjacent Maple Manor Cafe. 2507 S. Hastings Way (U.S. 53). (715) 834-2618.

Out to Eat

CHIPPEWA FALLS

Lindsays on Grand. Good spot for homemade food in a fast and friendly environment. These pies, soups, and sandwiches will bring you back again. 24 West Grand Avenue. (715) 723-4025.

Water's Edge Supper Club. Popular spot reached by boaters on Lake Wissota. Tie up your yacht or canoe at water's edge (or come by car). Standard supper club favorites like prime rib and seafood, but what's different here is a nice choice of Chinese entrees. On County S, five miles east of U.S. 53. (715) 723-0161.

EAU CLAIRE

Acoustic Cafe. The name comes from the fact that this is the place to be for live music on weekends. Their motto: "Let no one hunger for lack of a better sandwich." With that said, the sandwiches are good, the soups hearty, and the cafe atmosphere fun and inviting. 505 S. Barstow Street in the downtown area. There's also an Acoustic Cafe in downtown Menomonie. (715) 832-9090.

Camaraderie. For 50-plus years this popular place has been serving up good pub fare, including burgers, steaks, and "battered cheese curds." A favorite spot with University of Wisconsin-Eau Claire students. Open late morning to late evening. 442 Water Street. (715) 834-5411.

Dakota Grill. You don't have to go to Arizona to get your mesquite-grilled steaks. The next time you're in Eau Claire, stop by the Dakota Grill. Steaks, burgers, chicken, and ribs are grilled to perfection over a mesquite fire. 1720 Harding Avenue. (715) 839-7322.

Draganetti's Ristorante. One of Eau Claire's favorite places to eat Italian. You can't go wrong when you know three generations of family members have contributed to the menus. Dine in or carry out. Clairemont Avenue, one block east of U.S. 53. (715) 834-9234.

Maple Lounge & Cafe. To-die-for chicken-dumpling soup and other hearty, homemade goodies. You'd think maple was the first word in the English language the way the loyal patrons order up maple breakfasts here. 2507 S. Hastings Way. (715) 834-2618.

Mike's Smokehouse. Don't leave Eau Claire without first trying the Texas-style barbecued chicken, pork, and ribs, methodically cooked over a hickory pit. 2235 N. Clairemont. (715) 834-8153.

Northwoods Brew Pub. Eau Claire's first pub to brew its own beer. Full range of menu choices for lunch and dinner. Brewery tours available. 3560 Oakwood Mall Drive. Look for the Oakwood Mall Marquee. (715) 552-0510.

Sammy's Pizza. Back in the 1950s Sammy's was Eau Claire's first pizza parlor. And it's still going strong with its homemade pizza sauce and dough. Regulars say it's the best pizza in town. Pasta entrees and an Italian buffet are other offerings. 416 S. Barstow Street. (715) 834-5565.

MENOMONIE

Cafe Del Sol. Steaks, seafood, and sandwiches in a pleasant atmosphere. 1516 Thunderbird Mall. (715) 235-1941.

Cafe Matisse. Wonderfully inventive creations, especially the Portobello Mushroom Wellington, accompanied by sinfully rich desserts, California wines, and great coffee. 336 Main Street. A short walk from the Mabel Tainter Theater. (715) 235-4962.

Osseo

About 25 minutes southeast of Eau Claire and about a mile off I-94, get off the road and take a break in Osseo. One legend says that Osseo is a name in Henry Wadsworth Longfellow's poem *The Song of Hiawatha*. But another legend has it that when Native Americans first came over the hills of north-western Trempealeau County, they were so taken with the views that they cried out "Ah-See-Oh." Whatever the source for the name, from the 1850s on, Osseo has been the name for this pleasant community

Early white settlers were mostly Scandinavians, a remnant of history that visitors note still runs strong in the community's cultural heritage. Local shops sell Scandinavian clothes and gifts, while restaurants politely tell out-siders about lutefisk and lefse.

Lodging

Budget Host Ten Seven Motel. Modest motel caters to families. Ask about family rates. Yes, your family pet is welcome. At U.S. 10 and I-94. (800) 888-2199 or (715) 597-3114.

Osseo Camping Resort. Nature trails, hayrides, swimming pool, and playground. Open early April through end of November. 50483 Oak Grove Road. (715) 597-2102.

Park Motel. Unassuming place downtown—apartments and kitchenettes available. Friendly folks. Junction of U.S.10 and U.S. 53. Eight blocks after Exit 88 on U.S. 10. (715) 597-3721.

Rodeway Inn Alan House. Comfortable rooms in convenient location. Cocktail lounge and continental breakfast for guests. At U.S. 10 and I-94, Exit 88. (800) 453-4511 or (715) 597-3175.

Out to Eat

Norske Nook. In case you've never been to these parts, remember the name, Norske Nook Restaurant and Bakery. This pies-to-die-for spot happens to be one of the Midwest's favorite places to stop and eat with travelers near and far. In 1972 Esquire magazine said it was one of the country's 10 best spots for roadside food. There have been plenty of other accolades for this restaurant, including national TV coverage. But what it gets down to is that the Nook knows how to serve good home-cooked food in a friendly atmosphere.

If you miss Osseo, there are branches of the restaurant in Hayward and Rice Lake, but there's something about this Osseo location that has drivers dreaming about pies as they motor to it on the Interstate. The restaurant is so popular that it has an "overflow" restaurant directly across the street. So when you're looking for the Norske Nook in downtown Osseo, you'll see two of them. The newer establishment is usually open longer hours.

This restaurant knows how to whip up good old-fashioned recipes and, of course, pies. On a place mat heralding a Scandinavian rosemaling design, 16 types of pies dare you to resist. These are the daily choices: banana cream, butterscotch, rhubarb, apple, raspberry, chocolate, custard, sour-cream raisin, coconut cream, pecan, blueberry, lemon, and pumpkin. There are also three seasonal favorites: cherry, mincemeat, and fresh strawberry. Here's something else you should know: the meringue-topped pies are so high, you wonder how you'll find a way to get a piece in your mouth.

What else do they serve besides pies? Everything you'd expect on a breakfast, lunch, and dinner menu. Tip: If you're here before 10 A.M., Monday through Thursday, the coffee is only 40 cents. 207 West 7th Street, Osseo. (800) 294-6665 or (715) 597-3688.

Shopping

Dona's Ethnic Crafts. Another reason to visit Osseo is this shop, across the street from the new Norske Nook. Dona Krienke has been gathering exquisite arts and crafts for years, including magnificent tapestries (intricate reverse-appliqué work) from the hands of Hmong artisans who settled in the area from Laos. Dona also has for sale gorgeous Amish quilts from approximately 40 area Amish families. The shop is a virtual melting pot of cultures from around the world. Shoppers enjoy browsing through beautifully handmade items including a large selection of those famous Norwegian Dale sweaters, Scandinavian rosemaling and hardanger, and linens and gifts from Austria and Germany. 205 West 7th Street. Open Monday through Saturday. (715) 597-3765.

Many Little Things. This mini-mall contains, as the name says, many things, from Amish furniture, to glassware, stained glass, antiques, rare books, and handmade arts and crafts. Downtown Osseo. 216 West 7th Street. (715) 597-2879.

St. Croix River Valley

From Eau Claire, take I-94 northwest until you're about to cross a bridge into Minnesota. This is the town of Hudson, set on the Lower St. Croix River. If you want to see where the St. Croix meets the Mississippi River, go a few miles farther south to Prescott. Farther north, above the town of St. Croix Falls, the river is called the Upper St. Croix, which occasionally becomes a rushing torrent of water, particularly where it links up with another wild river, the Namekagon. The Lower St. Croix, by contrast, is its calmer cousin.

In 1968 the St. Croix Wild and Scenic Riverway System was the first to be designated by Congress as one of the country's wild rivers. Over 100 years ago this was one of the most important waterways in the Great Lakes, rivaling the Mississippi River in commercial traffic.

If you drive into the St. Croix River Valley, you may pass through Somerset, at the intersection of WI 35 and 64. If you come during the summer, you'll quickly see why the town is known as the Tubing Capital of Wisconsin. It's hard to ignore the busloads of visitors on their way to the Apple River to test its waters.

The towns of the St. Croix River Valley are filled with quaint bed and breakfast inns, historical sites, antique shops, and artists' studios. This area is a favorite hangout for artists, and consequently it is home to many arts organizations. On the other hand, outdoor enthusiasts have no reason to complain. The area is dotted with hundreds of lakes, streams, and parks. One attraction that shouldn't be missed is Interstate Park, the state's first official state park. Near St. Croix Falls, it's a magical place brimming with rock "characters." For more outdoor fun, take advantage of the opportunity to hike the Ice Age Trail.

If you come into this area without an agenda and want to find out what to see and do, you might want to start your exploring at the Polk County

Vistor Center in St. Croix Falls Here you'll find plenty of ideas for lodging, restaurants, entertainment, and enjoying the lush countryside. See the section on St. Croix Falls later in this chapter for more information.

Hudson

This charming old riverboat town has been able to do what many towns haven't—maintain its spirit of yesteryear. The steamboats are long gone—the harbors and open waters are now dotted with a plethora of sailboats. Yet it's easy to imagine how the area must have looked when the fur traders regularly came through in the early 1800s. In 1840, two traders, Peter Boushea and Louis Massey, named the town Willow River, a name that lasted eight years. It's interesting how names of Wisconsin towns often changed in their infancy. Sometimes, names were changed for no reason other than a settler wanting a name more to his liking.

That's what happened in Hudson. When Joel Foster settled here in 1848, he proclaimed Hudson to have the most beautiful views around. So the name changed to Buena Vista. There would be one more name change for this stunning settlement on the St. Croix River. A. D. Gray, the town's first mayor, said the St. Croix reminded him of the Hudson River in New York. The name stuck and, today, visitors who have marveled at the Hudson River Valley in New York can understand the comparison.

By the early part of the twentieth century, Hudson had become a busy railroad crossroads for businesses transporting goods back and forth to market in the Twin Cities. As Hudson thrived, it became a booming transportation center. Evidence of this is the Hudson Toll Bridge, which became a reality in 1913. Built by the Hudson Bridge Company and in use until 1951, it was the first toll bridge across the St. Croix River. Some interesting trivia: The toll for horse teams crossing the bridge when it first opened was 15 cents.

Today, the arch to the old bridge's entrance stands at First and Locust Streets. When the bridge was no longer used after 1951, its lights were extinguished but not permanently. Through the efforts of concerned citizens, the arch has once again been lighting up the area since 1995. Take a walk out on the bridge, even though it no longer spans the entire width of the St. Croix River, as another way to experience the area.

Hudson has a number of historical spots, including many turn-of-the-century homes now doubling as bed and breakfast inns. This is one interesting place for soaking up the character of the area. **For more information, call the Hudson Area Chamber of Commerce and Tourism Bureau, (800) 657-6775.**

Sights and Attractions

The Octagon House. Built in 1855 and listed in the National Register of Historic Places, the eight-sided house with its belvedere tower (climb to the third-floor tower and take a look at toys and other memorabilia) was built for Judge John Moffat and his family. Interestingly, four generations of Moffats lived in the house before the St. Croix County Historical Society bought it in 1964. The main house offers an intriguing insight into a different world. Note the pattern on the red velvet tablecloth in the living room. A Victorian entrepreneur thought this up—the intricate design is ironed onto the fabric. In the dining room, on the back of each piece of the gold-rimmed Haviland china, the inscription reads, "Made for the Phipps family. Christmas, 1919." The Phipps's were the well-known lumber baron family that lived across the street. Behind the main house is a garden and carriage house furnished with Victorian furnishings and accessories. 1004 Third Street. Open May through October, Tuesday through Saturday, 10-11:30 A.M. and 2-4:30 P.M.; Sundays, 2-4:30 P.M. (715) 386-2654.

Willow River State Park. 2,800 acres of forest abundant with lakes and waterfalls. Hiking trails, boat launch, boathouse, and campsites. County A, off I-94. (715) 386-5931.

Tubing. Tubing goes on all summer at Apple River Campgrounds, 15 miles north of Hudson in Somerset, (715) 247-3378 or (800) 637-8936. In winter, tube down the slopes of the snow park at Badlands Recreation. About six miles east of Hudson on Badlands Road. (715) 386-1856.

Event

St. Croix Music and Art Festival. This exciting three-day jamboree at the end of July brings together artists, musicians, and craftspeople from all over Minnesota and Wisconsin. The setting at Lakefront Park offers many spots for picnicking while you enjoy the music. At this entertainment extravaganza, you'll also find unusual curios and art. Take the didjeridoo, an Australian aboriginal musical instrument I bought from Russ Mattson, an artisan from Stockholm, Wisconsin. This five-foot black and green beauty draws attention and makes interesting sounds. Downtown Hudson on the St. Croix River. Call the festival hotline. (800) 657-6775.

Lodging

Comfort Inn. Comfortable accommodations with heated indoor pool and whirlpool. Suites come with microwave and refrigerator. 811 Domion Drive. (800) 228-5150 or (715) 386-6355.

The Grapevine Inn. A fine Victorian country inn built in 1901 for the legendary Hans Andersen, a Danish immigrant who founded Andersen Window corporation, the largest window manufacturer in the world. Note the luscious names of these guest rooms: Chardonnay and Emeralds, Bordeaux and Buttercream, and Champagne and Roses. Antiques galore, beautiful stenciling, lots of pampering here. Outdoor heated pool. 702 Vine Street. (715) 386-1989.

The Holiday Inn Express Hotel and Suites. Amenities include pool, hot tub, sauna, whirlpool, and exercise room. Continental breakfast. 1200 Gateway Blvd. (715) 386-6200.

Phipps Inn. A magnificent lumber baron's mansion in the heart of town. Breakfasts come with the trip back to yesteryear. 1005 Third St. (715) 386-0800.

Out to Eat

The Daily Grind. Salads, soups, sandwiches, outstanding breads, and coffee. Dine in or carry out. 432 Second Street. (715) 381-2775.

Mama Maria's. What else but authentic Italian cuisine. 708 Sixth Street North. (715) 386-7949.

Hudson Country Club. A good spot to go for Friday night fish fries. Also open for lunch. 378 Frontage Road. (715) 386-6515.

JR Ranch Steakhouse. Grill your own steak to your heart's content. Popular meeting place for breakfast, lunch, and dinner. Off I-94 at U.S. 12, Exit 4. (715) 386-6190.

Osceola

North of Hudson and 45 minutes from the Twin Cities, Osceola (as well as other towns such as St. Croix Falls and Taylors Falls in Minnesota) once attracted so many Norwegian immigrants, the local paper reported, "Norwegians are coming in such large numbers, they're becoming as thick as blackberries."

Osceola's Cascade Falls are accessible via this wooden staircase, just off Main Street.

When settler and town founder William Kent saw the area's magnificent falls, he envisioned harnessing the water to power a sawmill. The name of the town at the time was Leroy, named after another early resident. But Kent wanted a name change, and he had the power to effect it because, by 1855, he owned a large tract of land that would later become part of the town. So he did what any clever businessman would do. He traded two sheep to Leroy in exchange for renaming the community. The name chosen was Osceola, the name of an Native American chief.

In the late 1800s, Osceola was a frequent steamboat stop. Passengers came to look at Cascade Falls, where Osceola Creek blends with the St. Croix River. Today, visitors do the same. Just a few feet from Main Street, in the heart of town, take the wooden steps down to the river's edge. Or you can get a good look at the falls by standing on the wooden staircase not far from Main Street's sidewalk.

When you're in downtown Osceola, it won't take you long to find humor and small-town charm. When I was there, displayed in the window of a Main Street restaurant was the quote of the day: "The best way to get your tomatoes to ripen is to go on vacation." As you get closer to the bluffs along the banks of the St. Croix River, you'll pass the lovely four-steepled Methodist church (built in 1854) on Third Street.

If you've traveled to Europe and enjoyed its small country inns and hotels, often tucked away off the beaten track, you should head for the **St. Croix River Inn** bed and breakfast in Osceola. In the early 1900s, the inn was created from magnificent rocks taken from, just a stone's throw away (couldn't resist that), the quarry south of town. As soon as you step inside, if you can take your eyes off the breathtaking views of the river below, examine the

Near the bluffs of the St. Croix River is the elegant old Methodist church.

wood and stone frame around the doorway. The wood has been meticulously cut, in a zigzag fashion, to fill in next to the rocks (similar to a reverse form of "chinking" found in old log buildings).

There's an intriguing bit of history in the lobby, which also doubles as a great room for relaxing and reading. If you have any doubt about Osceola doing its part to keep the lumber business alive 100 years ago, take a look at the Osceola Historical Society Calendar that is among the great room's reading and reference material. The March photo depicts an astounding 36,600 pounds of timber piled sky-high on a sled pulled by only four horses.

But of course you've come to do more than examine the architecture and reading material. Relaxing is easy here. All the suites are named for riverboats built in Osceola. There were 10 built here between 1853 and 1887, and the inn's seven rooms reflect the finest of the ships. All rooms are elegant, filled with antique reproductions, such as armoires holding TVs and a collection of recent magazines. Some suites have beds so high you need footstools to ascend. All guest rooms offer a stereo cassette, private baths, and a Jacuzzi.

My room, the Maggie Reaney (named for the largest boat constructed in Osceola), does not face the water and is perhaps the most modest of the inn's suites. Yet, this ultracozy nook, with its tiny print wallpaper, Currier and Ives

Osceola's St. Croix River Inn combines riverboat history with an elegant country inn setting.

prints, and four-poster bed, was ideal. If you want to spread out in more spacious surroundings, the Osceola suite may be your best bet. In fact, it's a favorite with honeymooners. This is more like an apartment over the water. The bed faces the panorama of the river, has a fireplace, wet bar, kitchen, and cozy dining area—there's even a grill outside on the patio for cooking out.

There's no doubt that this is a special place. Not many inns serve breakfast in the rooms, but here that comes with the territory. A superb breakfast that may include French toast, cranberry muffins, a bowl of sliced kiwi, juice, and a pot of freshly brewed coffee, is the norm here.

Sights and Attractions

Osceola Historical Society. Connect with the helpful folks here to find out what Osceola's most interesting old homes and landmarks are open to the public. One is the historic Emily Olson House (open June through October and also the home of the Historical Society) at 408 River Street, another is the Osceola Depot (open Memorial Day through October) in the heart of town. (715) 294-2480.

Osceola and St. Croix Valley Railway. Authentic steam and diesel locomotives pull vintage trains through the St. Croix River Valley. Special excursions and a variety of itineraries. Good time to ride is in the fall when the valley's splendid palette of colors is at its peak. Trains leave from the restored Osceola Depot, Saturdays, Sundays, and holidays, late May through October. (800) 711-2591.

Event

Wheels and Wings. This early-September festival offers an intriguing combination of events. It includes a collectible car show (hundreds of old-time cars), air show and fly-in, radio-controlled airplane demonstrations, plus an arts and crafts fair. Hard to beat that blend of interesting categories. Free shuttle between locations. (715) 755-3300 or (800) 947-0581.

Several shops and restaurants line Osceola's picturesque Main Street.

Shopping

Osceola's **Main Street** is home to many interesting shops. Among the potpourri is Old Mill Stream, a charming gift, book, and antique shop. You can't miss it. Look for the nine-foot Osceola chief at the entrance.

Dresser

Part of Dresser's claim to fame is that it (with about 650 residents) is purported to be the smallest Wisconsin village to own and support a public library. Originating in 1935 by the Women's Club of Dresser, the library is still going strong, now under the auspices of the Polk County Library Federation.

Dresser (settler Sam Dresser named it) grew up around the railroad, but that growth didn't guarantee that there would be an onslaught of settlers. The population in 1919, for instance, was 326, about half of what it is now. Since 1950, Dresser has been a name on the map for winter—sports enthusiasts associate the town with the nearby Trollhaugen Ski Area.

111

Sights and Attractions

Seven Pines Lodge. A century ago, Charles Lewis, a multimillionaire grain broker, was shocked to find that the logging industry had come close to cutting a stand of virgin white pine near the logging towns of Luck and Milltown in Polk County. Lewis bought the 680 acres for $8,000 in order to preserve the prized timber. Businessman that he was, he also wanted to build a place where visitors could stay and enjoy the area's mystical beauty. In 1903 he built Seven Pines, a lodge named after the seven magnificent pines standing sentry nearby. Today, the historic log lodge, built entirely by hand, with only square wooden pegs—no nails—is on the National Register of Historic Sites. The building, in the midst of a mesmerizing forest where a few of the original seven pines still stand, is presumed to be about 300 years old.

The rugged grandeur of the lodge has drawn visitors to fish the trout stream on the property (rent Stream House to see how it feels to live above a stream) ever since the lodge opened its doors. There were, at last count, around 5,500 brook and brown trout per trout-stream mile here. Visitors who come to this serene spot are looking for relaxation and terrific fly-fishing, and they find both. And perhaps that's why the lodge has hosted rich, famous, and powerful dignitaries over the years, including President Calvin Coolidge when he was in the White House.

Seven Pines Lodge, near the town of Lewis and the Gandy Dancer Trail.

I have visited Seven Pines a few times over the years, and each time its enchantment grows. On my last visit I was taken by a simple 1903 calendar (the year the lodge was built) I saw hanging on a wall as I walked in. When I spied that date, I once again felt as if I had entered a time warp, a place frozen in time.

The Seven Pines serves year-round gourmet dinners which are open to nonguests by reservation. The Sunday I visited, brunch featured all-you-can-drink champagne and a huge variety of unusual offerings, including partridge with morel mushrooms. Later, I strolled the grounds and watched wooden elves carved from tree trunks peeking out from behind pine trees. There is a quiet harmony here. It's easy to get close to nature, particularly if you're fly-fishing (lessons are available) in the stream.

There are five rooms in the main lodge, the Gate House Cabin (Lewis's original office), and the Log Bungalow, which has four spacious suites. From Frederic, go north on WI 35 for about five miles to Lewis. Turn right on 115th Street. (Oddly, the street numbers around here are unusually high.) After less than a mile, turn left onto 340th Street. Go about a half mile to Seven Pines gate. (715) 653-2323.

Troll made from a tree trunk at Seven Pines Lodge.

Trollhaugen Ski Area. This family-oriented ski area, with 100 percent capability for making snow, has 22 runs, two quad chairs, one double chair, and seven rope tows. One of the oldest established ski areas in the state, Trollhaugen has been going strong since 1950. All of its 80 acres are lit for night skiing. There's a ski school for both kids and adults, a separate snow park for snowboarding, live "trolls" on hand to greet the kids, and full ski and snowboard rental shop. A day ticket is good for skiing up to 10:00 P.M. Children under six ski free when accompanied by a adult skiers. Ski season runs from mid-November to April. The chalet's Royale Christie Restaurant is open year-round for breakfast, lunch, and dinner. You shouldn't miss the famous 16-foot salad bar with over 60 salad choices. Waiting for a skier to finish a run? Enjoy a cocktail or some downtime in front of the lodge's great stone fireplace. All major credit cards accepted at the ski area. On County F, east of Dresser about three-quarters of a mile. (715) 755-2955.

Out to Eat

Murphy's Bar and Grill. Large facility with a party and sports atmosphere. Volleyball courts, broomball courts, live music, and dance floor. Nice selection of hearty fare includes steaks, chicken, and pizza. 201 WI 35 in Dresser. (715) 755-3500.

St. Croix Falls

St. Croix Falls, population about 1,700, is the gateway to many outstanding outdoor recreational areas. It is also adjacent to Taylors Falls, Minnesota, about a mile away across the St. Croix River.

One of your first stops should be the **Polk County Visitor Center**. Built in 1993, this beautiful center is brimming with information on the area, but the surprise is the way you can process the information here. It's easy to lose track of time sitting in the center's comfortable chairs reading all that material. This place is a cross between a small museum and library, with wonderful old black-and-white photos of the area adorning the walls. Then there's the map of the world with countless arrows indicating where the center's visitors have come from. On WI 35, next to the well-known Dalles House motel and restaurant. (800) 222-POLK.

Sights and Attractions

Gandy Dancer Trail. This 98-mile hiking, biking (and mountain biking), and ATV trail begins in St. Croix Falls, then travels north to Superior. The trail follows in the path of railroad tracks that had been used for over a century, most recently by Minneapolis, St. Paul, and Sault Ste. Marie railroads.

Why the name gandy dancer? Years ago, many of the tools used to build and keep railroad tracks up and running were made by Chicago's Gandy Tool Company. Some of the railroad laborers went about their work in a kind of chorus line. While they sang and swung their picks and shovels, they moved in synchronized gyrations, and they eventually came to be known as gandy dancers.

What else is unique about the Gandy Dancer, which is often referred to as the "most user-friendly trail in the Midwest." It meanders through several small towns, each one offering restaurants, accommodations, or other conveniences, just a few miles apart from each other. For instance, from St. Croix Falls to Centuria, the distance is only four and a-half miles, and from Milltown to Luck, the distance is a little more than three and a-half miles. The trail is well marked with mileage signs so it's easy to pick a section and then get off and stop in one of the small towns for a break.

The trail is also geographically divided according to use. The southern half, from St. Croix Falls to Danbury, covers 47 miles. Here, the crushed-rock base offers opportunities for hiking and biking, April through November. You'll need to get a bike pass for riding the trail.

On the northern stretch of the trail, covering 52 miles from Danbury, through parts of Minnesota, then to Superior, the landscape is wilder. Hiking, mountain biking, and ATV riding are allowed from April through November. From December through March, both the north and south sections are open for snowmobiles and ATVs. The Wisconsin section of the trail is run by the Burnett County and the Polk County Parks Departments. **Burnett County**

Tourism. (800) 788-3164. Polk County Information Center. (800) 222-POLK.

Ice Age Trail. The Ice Age Trail runs for 475 miles as it zigzags across the state tracing Wisconsin's world-famous glacial landscape. The evidence of this glacial movement is so well preserved in Wisconsin that in 1964, Congress passed legislation to protect the the Ice Age Trail in the state. Each part of the trail tells a unique chapter of the story of the glaciers. For example, along the Pothole Trail, you can see how the astonishing gorges and rock formations were created by the terrific force of glacial meltwater.

Interstate Park and Ice Age Interpretive Center. What was the state's first state park? You'd be right if you said Interstate Park, situated along the southern edge of St. Croix Falls and along the St. Croix River. It was also the first park in the country situated in two different states (Wisconsin and Minnesota). One of the most important features of the park is the Dalles of the St. Croix River.

When lumbering was at its peak in the area between 1830 and 1890, the St. Croix was a major artery for getting timber to market. At one time, the Dalles of the St. Croix served as a holding area for more than 150 million board feet of logs—resulting in the largest logjam in the world. It took 200 lumberjacks working six weeks to break up the enormous log pile.

If you've been to Devil's Lake State Park near Baraboo or seen the glens and gorges in the Wisconsin Dells, you'll have an idea of what this cavernous park looks like. Steep gorges, magnificent rock walls, and intriguing rock formations are all reasons why visitors have gravitated here for the past 100 years. The park is open year-round and offers an outstanding number of opportunities for outdoor recreation. Camp, bike, swim, fish, boat, bike, take river trips, cross-country ski—you can do it all here.

If you'd like to know what Wisconsin was like when the great glaciers moved over the state, visit the Ice Age Interpretive Center in the park. Take in the educational displays, films, and exhibits. Open daily year-round. The park is open year-round from 6:00 A.M. until 11:00 P.M. (715) 483-3747. For camping reservations, June 1 to August 31, call (715) 483-3742.

Pothole Trail and Old Man of the Dalles. Over a billion years ago, lava flowed into the Lake Superior Basin to form layers, which are found throughout the northwestern section of the state. To add to this topography, four different glaciers came through here about a million years ago. About ten-thousand years ago, the last one covered the area; then, when it retreated, it left huge amounts of glacial melt on top of the lava layers. The result was this astonishing river gorge and its wonderful rock formations, through which the Pothole Trail meanders. Probably the most famous and sought after is the one called the Old Man of the Dalles. This oddity, resembling a huge head of a man watching the river below, is a favorite place to stop and take a picture. While the Old Man resembles its name, so do the Cross and Devil's Chair. These scene-stealers make excellent backdrops for canoeists who frequently paddle the St. Croix as it weaves through here.

Lodging

Dalles House. This popular spot's great location is convenient to local state parks and ski areas. The motel offers an indoor pool, sauna, and tanning spa. The Dalles House restaurant is a favorite place to linger over fine food like walleye, steaks, and ribs while enjoying the scenic views. One block south of the U.S. 8 and WI 35 intersection (near the Polk County Visitor Center). Restaurant: (715) 483-3246; Motel: (715) 483-3206 or (800) 341-8000.

Wissahickon Farms Country Inn. Rustic inn on the Gandy Dancer Trail features continental breakfast, whirlpool, and kitchenette accommodations. Open all year. 2263 Maple Drive. (715) 483-3986.

Out to Eat

Valley Family Restaurant. If you're a breakfast fan, here you can order breakfast items all day long. Boasting the largest breakfast menu in the area, the friendly restaurant serves hearty food to start the day, including terrific pancakes, plus other down-home selections, amid an atmosphere of striking Dalles photographs. A smaller selection of breakfast items is available throughout the day as well as lunch and dinner. The action starts at 6:00 A.M. Main Street, downtown St. Croix Falls. (715) 483-9902.

Frederic

A former logging village, Frederic has around 1,100 residents and offers many reasons to stop and spend time in the outdoors, for example the nine-hole Frederic Country Club. Frederic is a logical stop on the Gandy Dancer Trail, in addition to being near two other trail hikers' and riders' favorites—the Coon Lake and Trade River Trails.

Sights and Attractions

Coon Lake Trail and Trade River Trail. The 3.3-mile Coon Lake Trail follows part of the shoreline of picturesque Coon Lake. It has several high and low points, many loops, and a hairpin curve. The shorter, easier Trade River Trail meanders near the Trade River, then follows open, rolling fields. Both trails are ideal for cross-country skiing, skating, hiking, and biking. For trail conditions, call Frederic Village Hall (715) 327-4294 Monday through Friday.

Lodging

Birchwood Beach Campgrounds and Resort and Lakeside Trails and Stable. On lovely Spirit Lake, about 10 miles northwest of Frederic. The resort has 16 sites, plus four cabins. The lake is great for swimming and fishing (northern pike, bass, sunfish). Make a reservation and you can also go horseback riding or ride a hay wagon. 21710 Spirit Lake Road West. (715) 327-8965.

Frederic Motel. Conveniently located one mile south of WI 35 next door to the Frederic County Club. Pets okay. 807 Wisconsin Avenue South. (715) 327-4496.

Gandy Dancer B and B. Two guest rooms, the Agnes and the Ray, offer comfortable lounging in a cozy countryside home. If you want to sleep in a fine, old four-poster bed, ask for the Agnes. Full breakfast, reasonable rates. 3281 E. 150th Lane. (715) 327-8750.

Barron and Cameron

East of the St. Croix River Valley lies Barron County, the heart of the Indian Head region. With over 100 freshwater lakes and endless trout streams offering game fish, Barron County has fishing holes that compete with the best in the state. For those who want to get away from the hurley-burly, this uncrowded territory is the place to be. However, increasing numbers of travelers are discovering its uncommon rustic beauty and plentiful activities. Here are just a few of them.

The next time you think of turkeys, think of Barron, the county seat. The huge Jerome Foods operation, with 2,000 employees, has been producing turkey products here for more than 75 years; today the products are sold under the name The Turkey Store. Barron, southwest of Rice Lake on WI 8, is a thriving community of about 3,000. These residents have an exciting new reason to feel proud of their community. That's because of the Barron Area Community Center, an exceptional facility that houses a 500-seat theater, indoor swimming pool, racquetball courts, gym, weight room, and sauna. To find out more, call (715) 537-6666. **For more information about Barron, contact the City Hall. (715) 537-5631.**

Cameron is nestled at the junction of the county's two busy crossroads, U.S. 53 and U.S. 8. It also serves as the gateway to the Blue Hills and an impressive chain of six lakes. Most people probably know Cameron because of the its wonderful pioneer village (see below). **For more information about the town, call the Cameron Village Hall. (715) 458-2117.**

Sights and Attractions

Barron County Historical Museum. If you've been to Old World Wisconsin in the town of Eagle, southwest of Milwaukee, the Pioneer Village Museum may seem familiar. The farms at Old World Wisconsin, representing several ethnic groups, were moved from their original sites to the expansive grounds at Eagle. Here, 28 historic Barron County buildings were carefully moved in order for viewers to see how an pioneer village once operated. Browse through vintage shops, a church, farmstead, jail, school, and other buildings. The old gas station is a charmer. Open June through Labor Day (Thurs.–Sun.). Special events run at various times throughout the summer, including Heritage Days the first weekend in July and the antique and

117

modern quilt show on Labor Day weekend. Admission. One mile west of Cameron on County W. (715) 458-2080 or (715) 458-2841.

Chetek

Most visitors to Chetek, known as "the City of Lakes," come to play and hide out along the area's chain of six lakes. Chetek is a community rightly proud of its tourism—it's been a boon to the area for more than five generations. Looking for competitive fishing with thousands of dollars in cash prizes? Then show up here for the annual Chetek Fish-O-Rama. Fishing for tagged fish goes on all summer, starting at the opening of fishing season, the first Saturday in May. What are your chances of catching a tagged fish? In 1997, for example, 439 fish were tagged and placed in the Chetek chain— only 121 were caught that summer. Conclusion: the fish and money are waiting. **For more information about the competition and other local happenings, call the Chetek City Hall. (715) 924-4838.**

Lodging

Rainbow's End Resort. If you don't want to rough it, these furnished vacation homes offer TV, games galore, including table tennis and volleyball, and a swimming area with a water slide and raft. On Lake Chetek. 2626 N. McClurg-7 1/4 Avenue. (715) 924-3141.

Red Lodge Resort. Fifteen housekeeping cottages located on the chain of the Big Six Lakes. Each completely furnished cottage comes with a 14-foot boat. Children's playground, shallow beach. (715) 924-4113.

Wildwood Resort. One- to five-bedroom cottages in the woods. Outdoor swimming pool; boat rentals include pontoon and paddleboats. Lakeshore family resort open year-round. (715) 924-3259.

Rice Lake

The Red Cedar River, which flows through Rice Lake, is known to be an excellent fishing hole, particularly for bass. But, as the name implies, Rice Lake is also known for its abundance of old rice beds along the edge of Rice Lake and Lower Rice Lake.

Sights and Attractions

The Blue Hills. Ten minutes east of Rice Lake are the Blue Hills, an appropriate name given to them by the Woodland Sioux. On sunny days in particular, the ridges show off a sparkling sea-blue color. It's also interesting to note that these high hills are older than either the Rocky Mountains or the Appalachian Mountains, and they're also believed to have once been the highest mountains in North America. Carved from the massive glaciers that moved through here, they once had peaks of 20,000 feet. Today, you can enjoy the Blue Hills Trail, a densely forested trail ideal for hiking, biking, and cross-country skiing. Also in the Blue Hills is Christie Mountain, a downhill ski area with ten 4,000-foot-long runs.

Red Barn Theater. Productions run from June to September. The theater presents a variety of performances, everything from serious drama to slapstick comedy. Northeast of town on WI 48. (715) 234-8897.

Turtleback Golf and Country Club. A superb new course, awarded four stars by *Golf Digest* magazine. The play's the thing here, but the restaurant's culinary treasures have earned high marks as well. Casual and fine dining includes steak, seafood, pizza, and other favorite choices. One mile west on Allen Road. Pro Shop, (715) 234-7641; reservations, (715) 234-6607.

Event

Rice Lake Aquafest. The second week of June the entire community goes all out to celebrate Aquafest. Parades, more parades, art, food, and fun.

Out to Eat

Norske Nook. Just in case you missed its sister restaurants in Osseo, you've got another chance to try pies and other assorted goodies at this branch. This is a larger, airier restaurant than the two in Osseo, which makes for more comfortable dining, but this rendition somehow lacks the coziness of the Osseo Nooks. 2900 Pioneer Avenue. (715) 234-1733.

Shopping

Bear Paw Co. In the confines of one interesting location, you can shop for sporting goods and take in the stuffed polar bears and other assorted wildlife, all the while shopping for gifts you can't live without. At the junction of U.S. 53 and WI 48. (715) 236-7300.

Wisconsin Wild Rice Company. It would be a shame to visit Rice Lake without taking home some rice. This store sells wholesale and retail rice and happily ships what you can't carry. 29 West Marshall. (715) 234-4161.

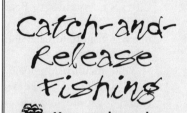

Catch-and-Release Fishing

Many anglers today fish for photographs, not trophy catches.

If you're not going to keep a fish you've caught because of its size or any other reason, here are the best ways to ensure that the fish will survive when you release it:

• Reel the fish in as quickly as possible.

• When removing the hook, keep the fish in water. If possible, use hooks without barbs.

• If the hook is deep and difficult to remove, cut the line and leave it in. It's surprising how many fish survive with hooks inside them.

• Don't give up on a fish that appears dead. The fish may be traumatized. Gently move water back and forth in the fish's gills so it can recover.

• Put fish back in the water near the spot you reeled it in.

Cumberland

Cumberland, west of Rice Lake on WI 48, is aptly nicknamed the Island City. It's surrounded by Beaver Dam Lake, the deepest lake in Barron County at 106 feet, and by more than 50 other lakes within a 10-mile radius. During one trip I spotted more great blue herons standing at these lakeshores than anywhere I'd been.

This small town has the feel of a bustling urban center—it is home to a two-year branch of the University of Wisconsin and has a fine airport facility and busy downtown shopping area (many specialty and antiques shops on Second Avenue). But it also has the contagious charm of a small northwestern Wisconsin town.

Hunters converge in the fall in the pursuit of ducks, small game, and partridge. Bow hunters, as well as gun enthusiasts, roam the countryside during hunting season. Another familiar scene on the landscape is the ice-fishing shanties dotting the frozen lakes in the winter.

In the summer there are plenty of vacationers patronizing area restaurants and shops, but this is not as much a resort town as it is a thriving place to work and live. There's one more thing about Cumberland you'll want to remember. If you like rutabagas, this is the place. Here, the lowly rutabaga has been lifted to exalted heights. For five days in late August, Cumberland celebrates the vegetable with a lively Rutabaga Fest. This event, filled with rutabaga cook-offs, fun runs, food, bands, and entertainment, has been going strong since 1932.

Sights and Attractions

Cumberland Golf Club. This 18-hole, par-72 course offers golfers of all abilities a chance to experience fun and challenging play. Cart rentals, driving range, and golf lessons available. Popular Friday night fish fry in the club restaurant. Two miles west of Cumberland just off WI 48. (715) 822-4333.

Lodging

The Rectory Bed and Breakfast. This marvelous structure, built in 1898 with a turreted facade on a small hillside, was once connected with St. Mary's Catholic Church next door. The church has since moved, but the quiet ambiance of the neighborhood remains. Four bedrooms. Easy walk to shops and parks. 1575 Second Avenue. (715) 822-3151.

Silver Pine Lodge. Log inn on scenic Silver Lake. Lots of things to do nearby, including golfing, antiques, swimming, and fishing. (715) 822-3123.

Out to Eat

5 O'Clock Club. The name assumes you know that fine gourmet dining starts here after 5 P.M. Located on lovely Granite Lake, the restaurant features an extraordinary menu of Italian, Chinese, European, and American specialties, including flaming table-side entrees and delectable desserts, all in a nautical environment matching the mood of the lake. Reservations recommended. 2639 7th Street. Don't let the street name confuse you into thinking this is a downtown location. Go about four miles north of town on U.S. 63, then watch for signs. (715) 822-2924.

Sammy's Pizza and Restaurant. This modest-looking place serves sensational made-from-scratch pizza, ravioli, and cavatilles. Also, spaghetti, sandwiches, beer, and wine. Off U.S. 63, across from the city beach. Closed Monday. (715) 822-4533.

The Spot Bar and Grill. If you like broasted chicken, this is where you should gravitate. Casual spot known for roast beef sandwiches, meatball sandwiches, and burgers. Open for lunch and dinner daily. In the middle of Cumberland on Main Street. (715) 822-4457.

The Tower House. Beautiful Queen Anne house with three-story tower offers fine American and Italian dining daily. Just when you thought you had your fill of smorgasbords, it's doubtful you've seen anything like the Italian spread offered here on Sundays. Downtown Cumberland. (715) 822-8457.

Turtle Lake

The town of Turtle Lake was originally named Skowhagen because it reminded an early settler, Joel Richardson, of the town he left in Maine before he set down stakes here in the mid-1800s. Later, there were so many turtles found in the lakes by local lumber companies that the present name was adopted when the first post office opened. The area is surrounded by a chain of lakes that includes Upper and Lower Turtle Lake, Horseshoe Lake, Echo Lake, Skinaway Lake, and Moon Lake. In midwinter, ice-fishing abounds.

Sights and Attractions

St. Croix Casino and Hotel. This attractive casino, set in a North Woods atmosphere and operated by the St. Croix Chippewa, offers a variety of gambling options 24 hours a day (you must be 21 years or older). The casino has more than 30 blackjack tables, 900 loose slots, bingo, and much more. No place to stay? The casino has taken care of that. Reserve a room in the adjacent 160-room hotel and enjoy a fine complimentary continental breakfast. 777 U.S. 8. (800)-U-GO-U-WIN.

Events

Turtle Lake Intercounty Free Fair. If you're in town the first weekend in July, take in a this multipurpose show, with a demolition derby, tractor pull, live entertainment, and a turtle race, of course. **Call the Turtle Lake Chamber of Commerce for more information about both events. 114 Martin Avenue. (715) 986-2241.**

Shell Lake

Talk to anyone from Shell Lake, the county seat of Washburn county, and you'll soon find out that the residents just love living here. That contagious spirit comes across in this small town south of Spooner on U.S. 63. Maybe it's because Shell Lake, the lake, which was named after the town (or is it the other way around?), would make anyone proud. The lake's beautiful crystal-blue waters make up the largest landlocked, spring-fed lake in the state. What can you do on Shell Lake? Fish for walleye, muskie, bass, or panfish, or go sailing. The lake is a favorite with sailors of all abilities.

If you can't get out in the woods in the early spring to tap your own maple syrup, then don't leave Shell Lake without samples of the local sweet stuff. The area is famous for its rich maple syrup and honey-producing apiaries. There is also good shopping in numerous gift and antiques shops.

Sights and Attractions

Clam River Golf Club. Nine-hole course with undulating greens. Club house has snack bar, golf club and cart rental, and pro shop. 1199 Hilltop Road, five miles west of Shell Lake on Sand Road; go left one mile, then right one-quarter mile. (715) 468-2900.

Schaefer Apiaries. While you shop for honey and maple syrup, you can watch the bees in the fascinating exhibits. U.S. 63, halfway between Shell Lake and Spooner. (Mid-April–Dec.) (715) 468-7484.

Shopping

Thunder Gift Gallery. If you can't get enough handmade jewelry and distinctive artwork, do what I did—give in to temptation and get more. It was hard to resist an out-of-the-ordinary hand-wrought bracelet from one of Bob and Diane Ericksen's buying trips. They comb northern Wisconsin and various spots in the western United States for artistic treasures. The Ericksens are well acquainted with the Shell Lake area and consequently double as its tourist information bureau. Open Monday through Saturday. Winter hours vary. 105 U.S. 63. (715) 468-4477.

Spooner

Spooner is a homey sort of place that, once you've been here a while, makes you realize that friendly spirit runs throughout the community. That attitude showed up each time I was drawn into the Spooner Bake Shoppe, whose friendly bakers have been baking award-winning cakes, breads, cookies, and pastries since 1952. They also create delicious sandwiches using their homemade bread. 217 Walnut Street. (715) 635-2643.

The Spooner area is close to 1,000 lakes and three rivers, including the exciting Namekagon River. Nearby there are also five golf courses and countless trails for hiking, biking, and skiing. **Spooner Chamber of Commerce. (715) 635-2168 or (800) 367-3306.**

Sights and Attractions

Railroad Memories Museum. If you're a train buff, you won't want to miss this nostalgic spot. Retired railroad professionals who volunteer their time here are happy to provide insights into this interesting collection of railroad paraphernalia. No train rides, but lots of fascinating information from those who know trains. Located in the old Chicago and North Western railroad depot in the downtown area. Open daily, Memorial Day through Labor Day.

State Fish Hatchery. This is the largest hatchery of its kind in the world. It annually produces 100,000 muskie and two million walleye and northern pike. To get a sense of how big the operation is consider that workers harvest about 25 million walleye eggs and 2 million muskie eggs annually. Watch fish being hatched in glass viewing tanks, peek at wildlife in the ponds, or take an easy stroll from the dam to the park, situated on the banks of the Yellow River Flowage. Open year-round, Monday through Friday. Near the junction of U.S. 63 and WI 253. (715) 635-4147.

Event

Spooner Rodeo. For over 45 years Spooner has played host to this world-class rodeo for three days in mid-July. Top U.S. cowgirls and cowboys compete for big money in events such as bull riding, bronco riding, steer wrestling, and team roping. Held at the Washburn County Fairgrounds behind the Country House Motel and IGA store. **Call the Washburn County Tourism Bureau. (800) 367-3306.**

Rustic Roads

In 1973, the Rustic Roads System was created by the Wisconsin State Legislature. The purpose was to preserve lightly traveled country roads so they might be long enjoyed by bikers, hikers, and car travelers. There are 67 rustic roads in the state, many of them in the northern portion of the state. In fact, the first rustic road so designated is R-1 in Taylor County, near Rib Lake.

When you see brown and yellow rustic road signs, you'll also see a number corresponding to where it is on the map. Booklets showing the road locations can be obtained at many visitor centers or through the Department of Transportation in Madison.

What distinguishes a road as rustic? It should have geographical as well as historical significance, striking terrain or native wildlife, be lightly traveled, and not less than two miles long. Rustic roads make excellent outings because they offer fairly short, wonderfully scenic drives, usually averaging about four miles in length. The maximum speed limit on a rustic road is 45 miles per hour.

Trego

The Namekagon River is the northern link to the St. Croix National Scenic Riverway, a wild and rugged waterway passing over 250 miles as it moves through Wisconsin and Minnesota. Trego, six miles north of Spooner, is at the Great South Bend of the river and consequently the area presents numerous opportunities for canoeing, tubing, water sports, and camping. One of the numerous outfitters is Namekagon Outfitters, on the Namekagon River at U.S. 63 and U.S. 53. They have a campground for those who want to spend more than a day on the water and a variety of river trips that include shuttle service. (715) 635-2015 or (800) 547-9028.

Birchwood

The unassuming small town of Birchwood is known primarily for its love of two things: bluegills and polka. Called the Bluegill Capital of Wisconsin, the town has been been celebrating its connection with bluegills for over 25 years by staging a down-home Bluegill Festival. It all happens the third weekend every June. Can't make it for that? No problem. They've got another festival coming up the following weekend that celebrates the townsfolks' favorite dance—the polka. **Birchwood Area Lakes Association. (715) 354-7846 or (800) 236-2252.**

Sights and Attractions

Tagalong Golf Resort. Three miles south of Birchwood, at the end of a long, winding road off WI 48, is one of the more interesting golf resorts in Wisconsin. It was built in 1923 by Frank Deming Stout, a director of the Chicago and North Western Railroad (his brother, James, was a Wisconsin senator who also founded the Stout Institute, now the University of Wisconsin-Stout). Stout had long been smitten with Scotland's legendary St. Andrews Golf Course and so, on the shores of Red Cedar Lake near Birchwood, he built his private golf estate using grass seed from Scotland and local boulders for the buildings. The name for the club came from one of Stout's favorite comic strips in the *Chicago Tribune*.

Today, you can stay in a variety of interesting buildings, including Stonehaven, a restored barn, the 21-unit Lockhaven, the Highland House with four apartments, and the Bunkhouse, a recently built group-oriented lodging with six bedrooms. Dining is exceptional with duck, prime rib, and shrimp as regular offerings. Golf, dine, or relax to your heart's content. 2855 Tagalong Lane. (715) 354-3458 or (800) 657-4843.

Lodging

Fred Thomas Resort. Lake homes and condominiums are part of this inviting resort on Lake Chetac. Fred Thomas retired from professional baseball in 1924, then decided to build his dream vacation home on the shores of one of the best bass-fishing lakes in the state. Playground, marina facilities, pier with slide. Box 196, West Birchwood. (715) 334-3761 or (800) 236-3761.

Stout's Lodge-Island of Happy Days. Designed after the legendary Adirondack camps, this 1912 retreat on a 26-acre island in Red Cedar Lake was also once owned by Frank Deming Stout. A marvel of historic elegance, it has fine dining, tennis, croquet, a billiard room, pistol range, and the oldest bowling alley in Wisconsin. Located at the intersection of WI 48 and County V, one mile north of Mikana. (715) 354-3646 or (800) 690-2650.

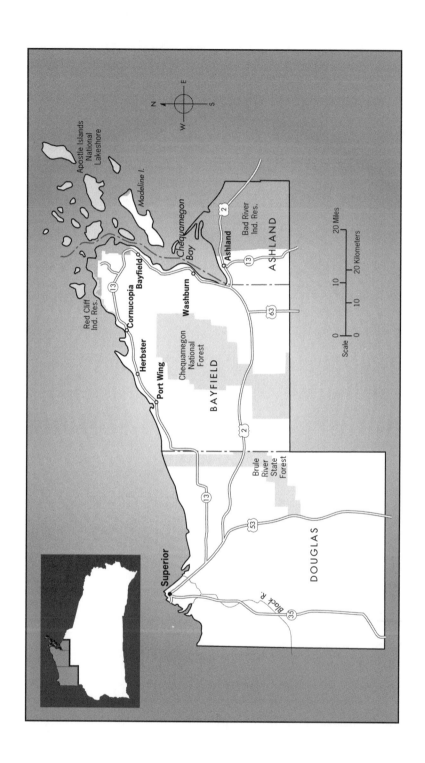

126

chapter 6

the Far Northwest—the Lake Superior Coastline

The spirit of northern Wisconsin is nowhere as prominent as it is in the northwestern region of the state. The area encompasses the coastline bordering the cool, deep waters of Lake Superior and a land rich with crystal-clear waters, tall pines and evergreens, and an ongoing commemoration of a rich heritage. The coastline communities continue to reflect their connection with the past. Commercial fishing, logging, shipping, quarrying stone, and railroading were the predominant industries long ago, while only fishing and shipping remain important to this region today. Although other industries, such as railroading, are mostly remnants of the past, their legacies remain strongly etched on the history of these communities.

Those who feel closest to this area understand its history. Some of its earliest inhabitants were the Ojibwa, who made the Great Lakes their home for thousands of years. Then, French, British, and Scottish fur traders discovered the area's riches and created transportation systems, trading posts, and villages throughout the area. Communities like LaPointe, on Madeline Island, sprang up along the coastline. All of these towns have an intriguing heritage that links them to the larger history of the majestic Lake Superior, the largest of the Great Lakes and the largest lake in the world.

You can learn more about the fascinating history of the area by visiting the Meteor Maritime Museum in Superior, the Madeline Island Historical Museum off the shores of Bayfield, the Historical Museum and Cultural Center in Washburn, and Ashland's Historical Society Museum. If you can't get to any of these, find out more about the area by talking to local residents. The coastline, sometimes ruggedly remote, keeps enticing new generations of adventurers who march to the beat of their own drum, in the same fashion as their ancestors. These rugged individualists are often direct descendants of the area's legendary pioneers. And for that reason, Wisconsin's Lake Superior coast has spawned a rich diversity of cultures and interests—not the least of which is its heritage of storytelling.

Superior

Superior has played an important part in the history of the state. Some would argue that the shape of the state resembles a crown (a stretch, but the point's well taken) and Superior is the crown jewel at its top. Jewel or not, Superior has some staggering statistics that can't help but impress you. For starters, it is the world's largest inland port, a distinction that comes from its endless array of ore docks, cranes, and "lakers." You'll hear the word *lakers* frequently around here, not in reference to the Los Angeles professional basketball team, but to those mammoth freighters plying Lake Superior's waters.

Along with being the world's largest inland port, Superior (and Duluth) is one of the busiest ports in the country. Because of the lake's great depth, sailors and freighter captains alike consistently call Superior the world's number one freshwater harbor.

What does this connection to water mean for a visitor? It translates to offering prime viewing areas for taking in panoramic water views. The best viewing area? Unmatchable vistas can be seen from Wisconsin Point, a four-mile-long sandbar outlining the harbor. More than a point of definition, this sandbar is home to a variety of trees that show off their flaming brilliance in fall—a good time to roam the beaches looking for water-smoothed agates or oddly shaped driftwood. Or just sit back and watch the ships edge through the shipping canal and past the picture-postcard lighthouse.

When you tire of sitting by the water, Superior has 21 parks waiting to be explored. The largest, Billings, has an attractive setting by the St. Louis River. Or you can always go across the bay to Duluth to explore the "other port" that makes this area a center of national and international shipping. **For more information, contact the Tourist Information Center, 305 Harbor View Parkway, next to Barker's Island, (800) 942-5313.**

Sights and Attractions

Amnicon State Park. The Amnicon River weaves its way through the scenic splendor of the park, making it an attractive spot for hiking, canoeing, cross-country skiing, or having a picnic. A quaint covered bridge, built in the 1930s, is a good place to take time out and ponder the landscape. Go ten miles east of Superior on U.S. 2, then north on County U for one-half mile.

Barker's Island. The center of Superior's and Duluth's efforts to revitalize the waterfront area, Barker's Island is the site of the S. S. Meteor Museum and where boat tours of the harbor begin; the island also has a marina, dining, and lodging. Off U.S. 2 and U.S. 53 near downtown Superior. Open mid-May to mid-October.

Brule River Canoeing and Kayaking. The Brule River, called the "River of Presidents" because Presidents Grant, Coolidge, and Eisenhower were drawn here by the exceptional trout fishing, flows through Blue River State Forest. Many sections of the river are fine for novice canoeists, yet advanced paddlers will find this a challenging waterway. Looking for something really different to brag about? Then sign up for a lake kayaking trip (a hot topic in these parts). You'll move along the Brule, then make your way 50 miles north out to Lake Superior. For more information call (715) 372-4983 (summer) or (715) 392-3132 (winter).

Harbor Excursions. If you don't have a boat of your own, reserve a spot on one of the Vista Fleet's three cruise boats for a narrated tour around the harbor. A rewarding way to take in ever-changing harbor views. Expect close-up looks at coal and ore docks, the largest grain elevator in the world, the shipping canal, and other area landmarks. Several tours each day leave from the Barker's Island docks. Lunch, dinner, and evening cruises throughout the season. Open May to October. (715) 394-6846 and (218) 722-6218.

Fairlawn Mansion and Museum. Once you arrive on Superior's waterfront, you can't miss this magnificent 42-room Victorian mansion with its skyscraping bell tower. Once the home of Martin Pattison, lumber baron and the second, third, and sixth mayor of Superior, the home was renovated by the Douglas County Historical Society in 1998. 906 East 2nd Street. Open daily. For tours and information, call (715) 394-5712.

Lake Nebagamon. 25 miles southeast of Superior, the village of Lake Nebagamon is a recreational mecca. The 950-acre lake draws visitors for water sports, while the woodland trails attract those who like to cross-country ski and ride snowmobiles. In the summer, catch music concerts in the log auditorium (it's not everyday you can say you were entertained in a log auditorium). 11484 E. Camp Nebagamon Drive. For more information, call (715) 374-2283.

Old Firehouse and Police Museum. What kid hasn't fantasized at least once about being a fireman or policeman? Here, kids and adults can vicariously find out what it was like to fight fires and crime at this authentic turn-of-the-century fire station, which includes antique police cars, fire trucks, a 1906 steam pumper, and other memorabilia. At 23rd Avenue and 4th Street, in Superior's East End. Open June to August. (715) 398-7558.

Pattison State Park. If you're tracking waterfalls, this is a must-stop. One of the park's illustrious highlights is Big Manitou Falls. At a height of 165 feet, it's Wisconsin's highest waterfall. The story goes that Gitchee Manitou, the Great Spirit, made a spectacle of himself by roaring through the Black River canyon, creating Big Manitou Falls in his wake. Besides watching waterfalls (Little Manitou Falls is a smaller version of its namesake), visitors come to swim, camp, hike, cross-country ski, and snowmobile. The park is 13 miles south of Superior on WI 35. Open year-round. (715) 399-3111.

S. S. Meteor Maritime Museum. Tour this whaleback ship, built in 1896, and the only one in existence today. The S. S. Meteor was a forerunner of today's 1,000-foot-long freighters, some of which you'll probably spot out on the harbor. The museum houses interesting exhibits and memorabilia centered around shipping on the Great Lakes. Visit in October and you'll find the ship has taken on a "haunted ship" visage. On Barker's Island. Open Memorial Day through early October. (715) 392-5742.

Events

The Great Northern Classic Rodeo. The Wild West meets northern Wisconsin on Labor Day weekend. Get to see roping, barrel racing, bull and bronco riding at its finest. Rodeo fans look forward to this rollicking event every year. At Head of the Lakes (HOL) Fairgrounds, 47th and Tower Avenue. (218) 726-1603.

Head of the Lakes Fair. Rides and stock car racing at the area's largest fair. Head to the Head of the Lakes Fairgrounds for action-packed fun. Fridays, May to September. (715) 394-7848.

Spirit of the Lake Fallfest. Various activities are planned each year, including arts and crafts fairs, sailing regattas, historic home tours, food, fun, and plenty of atmosphere as the leaves start showing gold and rosy colors. Mid-September. (715) 394-7716.

Lodging

Barker's Island Inn and Conference Center. Catch scenic marina views from the restaurant and lounge. Sports lounge, indoor pool, and whirlpool. Access to snowmobile and cross-country ski trails. Pets allowed. (800) 344-7515 or (715) 392-7152.

Best Western-Bay Walk Inn. Complimentary continental breakfast, indoor pool, whirlpool, sauna, and whirlpool suites. Pets allowed. 1405 Susquehanna. (800) 528-1234 or (715) 392-7600.

Best Western-Bridgeview. Complimentary breakfast bar. Indoor pool, whirlpool, and sauna. 415 Hammond Avenue. Pets allowed. (800) 777-5572 or (715) 392-8174.

Days Inn Bayfront. Easy access to snowmobile trails and skiing. Restaurant, indoor pool, whirlpool, game room, and sauna. 110 Harbor View Parkway. (800) DAYSINN or (715) 392-4783.

Out to Eat

Bob's Chop Suey House. Crazy about Chinese food but the rest of your family wants steak and chicken? No problem. Bob's features entrees such as chop suey and chow mein, as well as fried chicken and steaks. Dine in or carry out. Closed Monday and Tuesday. 1307 Tower Avenue. (715) 394-7272.

Bridgeman's Family Dining. If you love ice cream, then this is prime territory. Bridgeman's ice cream tradition has been going strong for over 100 years. Plenty of other favorites for breakfast (served all day), lunch, and dinner. Mariner Mall, Hill Avenue and 28th Street. (715) 392-1372.

Builders Saloon and Stargate Nightclub. Lively spot where the pub fare, while fine, is almost superfluous because the laser light show, karaoke, and mammoth TV screen are the main attractions. This is where those who like spontaneous combustion converge. 619 Tower Avenue. (715) 395-2222.

J. W. Beecroft Books and Coffee. A nice rendition of the popular books and coffeehouse theme. Soothe your mind and soul while you sip superb coffee in this delightful atmosphere. 3631 Tower Avenue. (715) 394-BOOK.

Library and Zona Rosa Restaurants. Hearty specialties include a huge salad bar and satisfying soups. Mexican food aficionados will appreciate this place. 1410 Tower Avenue. (715) 392-4821.

The Shack Smokehouse and Grille. Don't let that word *shack* throw you. Bring those you want to impress—the food's that good. Terrific steaks are served hot off the grill in a comfortable atmosphere, along with smoked barbecue, prime rib, and an assortment of seafood. 3301 Belknap Street, off the Bong Bridge. (715) 392-9836 or (715) 392-9837.

Town Crier Family Restaurant. Plenty of choices for all the family. Pancakes are a house specialty. Order breakfast any time of the day. 4927 East 2nd Street, U.S. 2 and U.S. 53 (next to the Super 8 Motel). (715) 398-7521.

Port Wing and Herbster

On Lake Superior's south shore, about 40 miles east of Superior on WI Highway 13, lies Port Wing, a charter-fishing center with a pervasive nautical charm. For an interesting stop, make your way over to the city park, where you'll find an odd assortment of memorabilia, including an old Wisconsin school bus, jail, and bell tower.

Further up the road on Highway 13 is Herbster, a quiet lakeshore community with good trout fishing and exceptional deepwater fishing. These two communities are good spots for getting away from the maddening crowds, enjoying a summer afternoon at a sandy beach, and watching the fishing boats go by.

Cornucopia

Further east along Highway 13 and on the far western end of the Apostle Island National Lakeshore, is the charming fishing village of Cornucopia, the northernmost community in Wisconsin. What do visitors find? A harbor with sandy beaches where they can buy fish right off the commercial fishing boats nearby, dramatic Squaw Bay caves, a good picnic area at Siskiwit Bay Park, and overnight camping at Lake Siskiwit just south of town. To add to the charm, some of the harborside fishing huts have been converted to interesting gift shops. St. Mary's Greek Orthodox Church, with its distinctive onion-domed canopy, adds to the picturesque landscape

Cornucopia also offers trails to Lost Creek Falls, along with hundreds of nearby groomed trails for hiking and snowmobiling. The community also has become a magnet for artists who want to live in a beautiful, unspoiled environment. There is also a handful of restaurants and lodging facilities.

Twenty miles northwest of Bayfield on WI 13, Cornucopia offers and an off-the-beaten-track experience that lingers with visitors for a long time after they've returned to more populous surroundings. Incidentally, the old stagecoach route between Bayfield and Cornucopia still exists, albeit the road is now paved. **For more information, contact the Cornucopia Business Association. (715) 742-3337, 742-3282 or 742-3994 (members of CBA).**

Lodging

Fo'c'sle Bed and Breakfast. Providing excellent views, the inn is located at Siskiwit Bay Marina, on WI. 13 at Superior Avenue. (715) 742-3337.

Out to Eat

Fish Lipps North Point Lounge and Restaurant. Good hearty food, and charter fishing too. 121 Superior Avenue. (715) 742-3378.

Shopping

Mosquito Farm Gifts and Accessories. Handmade gifts and accessories, stained glass, woodworking, among other offerings. On WI 13, one mile west of Cornucopia. (715) 742-3279.

Bayfield

About seven and a half hours north of Madison, far away from urban cares and suburban sprawl, is the tiny town of Bayfield (year-round population about 700), with its cobblestone streets and lovely old Victorian homes in a 60-block historic district. And the view from the windows of most of these will reveal a Lake Superior harbor scene as sparkling as you'll find anywhere in the state—or the rest of the country, for that matter.

In the 1400s, long before any Europeans made their way here, the Ojibwa were populating this unexplored area. They plied Lake Superior's waters and eventually settled on Madeline Island. Later, French and British adventurers arrived, and small settlements sprang up. But it wasn't until the late 1880s that Bayfield came into its own when commercial fishing began to prosper. The town's Boutin and Booth Fisheries found markets for its fresh fish all over the country. Whitefish are still a favored selection at local restaurants and fish boils; and, of course, whitefish livers are a popular local delicacy.

In the late 1880s, settlers found the Apostle Islands perfect for quarrying sandstone. Not surprisingly, the local quarry industry was born, as sandstone was cut and transported to booming cities around the country to satisfy their need for long-lasting building materials. Lumbering also flourished, and because of Bayfield's location, fruit farms and orchards thrived in the long growing season. Strawberries, blueberries, raspberries, apples, and pears still grow in abundance on local farms and orchards.

By the turn of the century, Bayfield saw a decline in its once thriving industries. Area waters had been overfished, the last sawmill closed, and a few decades later, the destructive sea lamprey invaded Lake Superior. Today, Bayfield has redefined itself. There are plenty of orchards, but tourism has become a booming business. Fortunately, for both tourists and residents, the town has retained its charm and character. Unlike some tourist destinations where every house, farm, barn, and gas station have been transformed into gift shops and art galleries, it hasn't happened here.

Bayfield's bustling harbor.

In 1997, after the *Chicago Tribune* searched for six weeks, traveled over 8,000 miles, and examined 139 towns looking for the "Best Little Town in the Midwest," Bayfield was given the top honor. Some people feared that all that publicity would spoil this no-stoplight, one-gas-station town (even though the Amoco station on Highway 13 is so appealing it could pass for a bed and breakfast). Sure, there were some quiet signs singing the praises of being number one (the Chamber of Commerce uses the phrase "Best Little Town in the Midwest" in some of its promotional material), but the good news is that all is well.

These friendly folks are still mighty friendly, and the town still looks like a poster for a northern paradise. For many, this is the end of the line for North Woods vacationers. With the exception of the Apostle Islands, you can't go farther north in Wisconsin than here. So far, Bayfield's undisturbed tranquillity remains intact. The one main road, WI 13, curls and winds through residential areas and, at every twist, opens up yet another glorious view of Lake Superior and its small armada of sailboats. What you won't find are big-name establishments like Burger King, Kmart, or Super 8. Bayfield has not yet been loved to death. **For more information, contact the Bayfield Chamber of Commerce, 42 S. Broad Street. (715) 779-3335.**

Outside the Thimbleberry Inn Bed and Breakfast in Bayfield.

Traveling to and from the communities around Bayfield is easy with BART, the local transportation system. This affordable bus system covers the corridor between Red Cliff, Bayfield, and Ashland. Buses shuttle passengers along this route throughout the day. And here's the best thing: just tell the driver where you want to get off and your wishes will be honored. To get on, just flag the bus down. In Bayfield, a favorite flagging-down area is at Gruenke's and Super Savers. Bus service runs year-round, Monday through Friday. (715) 682-9664.

Overlooking Lake Superior, the largest lake in the world by size (in terms of volume, the title goes to Russia's Lake Baikal), the setting of the **Thimbleberry Inn Bed and Breakfast** atop a lakeshore bluff is splendid. The inn was named for the wild thimbleberries growing on the inn's property. They look like thimbles and their taste is a cross between a cranberry and raspberry.

Interestingly, they're only grown in the Lake Superior area.

I had come to this beautiful contemporary retreat, built by owners Sharon and Craig Locey in 1992, to enjoy nature close up in a spectacular setting. My suite had a private entrance, wood-burning stove, and a comfy bed accented by an elaborate quilt made by artist Connie Daniel and inspired by scenes outside the inn. My suite, with floor-to-ceiling windows and a cathedral ceiling, had another bedroom in the loft above. Mornings start with Sharon bringing tea, hot chocolate, and coffee, plus freshly baked poppy seed muffins to each guest room (orange juice was already in my refrigerator). She encouraged me to take these goodies and sit on my "love seat" (an Adirondack chair) outdoors and enjoy the view of five of the Apostle Islands. (Each of the three guest rooms has a private retreat in the woods.)

Little did I know that these early-morning goodies were not the main event because 30 minutes later breakfast—the *real* breakfast—was announced. Sharon is an award-

The Thimbleberry Inn's guests have an opportunity to sail on the inn's 36-foot ketch, *Sandpiper*.

winning cook, and it showed in the morning's menu. On the dining room table, gigantic bowls of whipped cream and just-picked raspberries and strawberries stood ready to add to Sharon's perfectly baked puffy-apple pancakes. (Sharon's cookbook, *Cooking at Thimbleberry Inn*, shows her culinary versatility and is a great way to keep the memories of your stay here alive.)

Later, Craig, a licensed sailing captain and former U.S. Forest Service ecologist, took four of us on a half-day sailing venture on *Sandpiper*, his classic 36-foot wooden ketch (there's an additional charge for the trip). This magnificent sailboat was designed in 1930 but built much later, in 1978. Not only is it beautiful but also its interior design is so impressive that it was featured in the book *Classic Yacht Interiors*.

I could tell Craig was a master seaman (he started sailing at 11 and built his first boat at 12). Throughout the excursion he patiently explained how the boat's rigging worked. Fascinated by the onboard global positioning system, I became eager to take the helm. As we sailed around several of the Apostles I took a turn at the wheel. We passed rock ledges dotted with black cormorants and rocky shorelines covered with rare orange lichen. It was pure relaxation—yet another reason to head to Bayfield.

The Thimbleberry Inn's pier on Lake Superior.

Sights and Attractions

Lake Superior Big Top Chautauqua. If you don't hook up with one of the performances here during your stay, you've missed the area's artistic heart. In 1985, Big Top Chautauqua (BTC) was a dream of artistic director, founder, and writer-composer Warren Nelson. His vision was to bring together musical productions, theater, readings, storytelling, and Wisconsin's history of song to a family audience. The "house shows," or historical musicals, are the core of the BTC. The events are staged under a colossal canvas tent, which holds 750 patrons, in a valley at the base of Ashwabay Ski Hill. Set against the mountain, the Big Top, has a mystical, almost spiritual quality.

Every summer since 1986, from the beginning of June through early September, the Big Top has brought together entertainers like The Kingston Trio, Johnny Cash, Leo Kottke, Judy Collins, and Jacques Brel, as well as countless others. The performances are also heard on *Tent Show Radio*, a live variety series presented on Wisconsin Public Radio.

BTC is three miles south of Bayfield. Take WI 13 to Ski Hill Road, then follow the signs. A free shuttle service runs between Bayfield and BTC, and Ashland and BTC. Food and drinks are available at a snack bar. Performances every night, Tuesday through Sunday, early June through early September. Check performance times at (715) 373-5552 or (888) BIG-TENT.

Mt. Ashwabay Ski Area. Downhill ski area south of Bayfield at Washburn. Ski lessons available, as well as rentals. Thirteen downhill runs with a T-bar and rope tow, along with well-groomed 40 kilometers of cross-country ski trails. (715) 779-3227.

Red Cliff Isle Vista Casino. Owned by the Red Cliff Band of the Lake Superior Chippewa, the casino offers keno, reel slots, blackjack, and more. Spend time playing games or relax in the restaurant or lounge. Keep your ticket stub from the Big Top Chautauqua or Apostle Island Cruise Service to receive extra quarter tokens when you make your regular purchase of quarter tokens; the offer is usually good for a week after the date on the ticket stub. North of Bayfield on WI 13; at the sharp curve above town, look for the casino on the left. The Red Cliff also run another casino on Madeline Island. (715) 779-3712 or (800) 226-8478.

Events

Bayfield Applefest. You have to give credit to a small town like Bayfield for pulling in the numbers each year for this annual event— the largest apple festival in the state. Each year, over the first weekend of October, approximately 50,000 visitors descend upon the town's main streets. Every conceivable type of apple is featured, from the more common McIntosh and Cortland to the lesser-known varieties like Wolf River, Fireside, Dudley, and Hume. You can sample apples in everything, from apple pie, naturally, to apple mustard, and apple brats. The festival continues with apple bake-offs, street musicians, a strolling carnival, art and food booths, and a night parade of boats that eerily light up Lake Superior's waters. Tip: If you're planning to visit Bayfield during the Applefest, book your lodging months in advance.

Bayfield's Festival of the Arts. Put the fourth weekend in July on your calendar. That's when artists from Wisconsin, Michigan, and Minnesota gather at Memorial Park to show their paintings, glasswork, ceramics, jewelry, and more.

shakespeare Under the Big Top

The first time I took in a Big Chautauqua performance, the National Shakespeare Company was performing *Much Ado about Nothing*, and a most interesting evening it turned out to be. Rain started during the first act, then thunder crescendoed above the sound of the actors' voices. They were troopers though and maintained their composure throughout. During one scene, when the thunder and lightning were particularly violent and the tent flaps were snapping furiously, the actors never broke from character. The appreciative audience gave them thunderous (pardon the pun) applause. Then, to add to the surrealistic scene, several frogs hiding under the stage's canvas skirt made a run for it up the aisles. There was a lot to do about something here, making it a night to remember.

Blessing of the Fleet. Long ago hundreds of people used to gather on Bayfield's docks for the opening of the commercial fishing season, and to pray for a safe and successful harvest. The tradition began again in 1997 as a way to honor Bayfield's long connection with fishing and its venerable commercial fishing boats. Take in this unique event, usually during the second weekend in June, at the city docks.

Red Cliff Traditional Powwow. The Red Cliff Band of the Chippewa, also known as Anishinabe, "The Original People," hold their powwow each Fourth of July weekend. Everyone is welcome to the celebration, which features visiting royalty, sacred fire ceremonies, intertribal drummers, and dancers and singers from the Midwest and Canada. The powwow is held on the Red Cliff Reservation, which can be reached via County K off of WI 13 north of Bayfield. (715) 779-3700.

Bayfield's charming **Old Rittenhouse Inn.**

Lodging

Note that there are only about 500 guest rooms in Bayfield and on Madeline Island, accommodating about 1,300 visitors. If you're planning on staying in the Bayfield area on a summer weekend, make reservations early, in spring if possible.

Bay Front Inn. Several attractive inns hug the harbor near the city docks—this is one of them. Sixteen guest rooms, some with Jacuzzis, fireplaces, and decks. A nice continental breakfast comes with the territory. (715) 779-3880.

The Inn on Madeline Island. This 50-guest-room resort features tennis, a swimming pool, beach, golfing at the adjacent golf course, and a superb restaurant. In LaPointe. (715) 747-6315 or (800) 822-6315.

Old LaPointe Inn. If you want to be close to the harbor and museum on Madeline Island, this is your place. This 1870s inn is just a short stroll from the ferry dock and next to the museum. In LaPointe. (715) 747-2000.

Old Rittenhouse Inn. Set on a hill on Rittenhouse Avenue, this elegant Queen Anne mansion is one of the most photographed sites in Bayfield. In the summer, its wraparound porch becomes a garden of flowers; in winter, its wood-burning fireplaces keep the inn cozy. Hilltop location affords good views of Lake Superior a couple of blocks away. Twenty-one guest rooms with marvelous antiques. Distinctive gourmet lunch and dinners are open to everyone by reservation. 301 Rittenhouse Avenue. (715) 779-5111 or (888) 644-4667.

Silvernail Guest House. In 1887 the Silvernail brothers built this saltbox structure, where they opened a restaurant on the first floor and a photography studio on the second. Over the years the building has seen many uses. In 1993, Christine and Greg Carrier (a direct descendent of the Boutins, one of Bayfield's pioneer families) began restoring the property. Today, their efforts to achieve authenticity and charm are evident. In addition to five guest rooms, a courtyard suite with two adjacent guest rooms was added in 1996. Wonderful

Bayfield's historic Silvernail Guest House.

breakfast pastries and coffee make the stay even more memorable. A cross between a charming cottage and a museum. 249½ Rittenhouse Avenue, at the corner of 3rd Street. (715) 779-5575.

Thimbleberry Inn Bed and Breakfast. See the description on pages 134–136. 15021 Pageant Road. North of Bayfield, just south of Schooner Bay. Look for signs. (715) 779-5757 or (800) 881-5903.

Winfield Inn. This 31-unit motel complex has kitchenettes and beautiful views of the Apostle Islands. North of town, on WI 13. (715) 779-3252.

Out to Eat

Greunke's. Legend has it that this is the place that first served whitefish livers. Actually, frugal fishermen's wives didn't want to waste any part of the fish. So, fresh whitefish livers, deep-fried or sautéd, began showing up on local menus. Vic Gruenke is said to have put it on the menu, and the rest, as they say, is history. You'll find a good selection of seafood, steaks, and sandwiches at this popular spot. 17 Rittenhouse Avenue. (715) 779-5480.

Maggie's. If you can't get to Florida, this is your next best bet. This restaurant is easy to find—it's painted a bright pink and yellow—a tip-off to what's to come. Every conceivable size and shape of pink flamingo is hanging, nailed, framed, or displayed inside. The ceiling is loaded with flamingo memorabilia-in fact, the ceiling is filled with a lot of odd stuff, including a welcome mat. Their slogan, "Real food, real drinks, real fun, real catering, fake flamingos," sums it all up. Great charbroiled burgers and wild mushroom pizzas. 257 Manypenny. (715) 779-5641.

The pricey but wonderful **Clubhouse**, overlooking the golf course on Madeline Island, (715) 747-2612, and the festive **Egg Toss Cafe** (715) 779-5181, at 41 Manypenny Avenue, are under the same ownership as Maggie's.

Minnie's Coffee and Tea House. Opened in 1997, this place, set in a historic building a block up the hill from the harbor, is a perfect place to sip expresso or enjoy a scone. Also enjoy a variety of other fare, including freshly made soups and desserts. (715) 779-9619. 117 Rittenhouse Avenue.

Old Rittenhouse Inn. Visitors come from far and wide to take in the legendary culinary fare served for lunch and dinner. The creative regional specialties contain the best of Midwestern ingredients and are beautifully presented. True to restaurants serving imaginative cuisine, the menu changes often. A fine place to be pampered in a beautiful atmosphere. Reservations a must. 301 Rittenhouse Avenue. (715) 779-5111.

Wild by Nature Market. Not an in-house dining establishment, but not to be missed for terrific fast food. This vegetarian deli (new in 1997) was founded by three women who felt Bayfield lacked a good health food market. Their location is convenient, a block from the City Dock; so if you're going on an Apostle Islands cruise, take along some hearty food to eat on board. I enjoyed the California Wrap—Spanish rice, cilantro, black olives, avocado, mozzarella cheese, sour cream, and greens, all wrapped in a soft tortillalike shell. Also, chicken and turkey breast sandwiches, salads, bagels, dips, and spreads. 100 Rittenhouse Avenue. (715) 779-5075.

Shopping

The Bayfield area has an interesting variety of gift shops, book stores, art galleries, and antique shops. Here are two diverse samplings.

Joanne's Scandinavian. Billed as "the most complete Scandinavian store in the Upper Midwest," this homey shop is filled with Scandinavian gifts, home accessories, and clothes. An exceptional collection of Norwegian knit-

Joanne's Scandinavian, one of Bayfield's colorful shops.

wear, including the famous Dale sweaters. Also, hats, capes, and jackets. 223 Rittenhouse Avenue. (715) 779-5772 or (800) 297-5772.

20 North First Street. If you can't remember the name, look for the huge Statue of Liberty in the front yard. Antiques and collectibles galore. Wander to the shop's back room and lose time rummaging through wall-sized filing cabinets holding tons of interesting things such as cookbooks and decals. A good resource for finding oddities like full sets of Hardy Boys mysteries and Bobbsey Twins books. 20 N. First Street, across from Gruenke's. (715) 779-3909.

Apostle Islands National Lakeshore

The Apostle Islands National Lakeshore, composed of 21 islands and a 12-mile stretch of mainland, is home to a diverse population of wildlife and is one of the most picturesque and unspoiled regions in the Midwest.

In the 1960s, former Wisconsin governor Gaylord Nelson came to the Apostle Islands with President John F. Kennedy in hopes of encouraging him to push along national preservation of the area. Federal recognition finally came in 1970 when President Richard Nixon signed the papers making the Apostle Islands National Lakeshore a federally recognized sanctuary.

This national lakeshore contains more lighthouses than any other park in the national system: six. They were all built between 1857 and 1891. The

141

islands with lights are: Sand, Devils, Raspberry, Long, Outer, and Michigan. You can learn more about these islands and their lights at the Apostle Islands National Lakeshore Visitors Center in Bayfield. Or take the special lighthouse cruise or lighthouse/Squaw Bay Sea Caves evening cruise offered by the Apostle Island Cruise Service.

Here are some other interesting facts:

- The smallest island is Gull, with only three acres, and the largest is Stockton, with 10,000 acres.
- Tours of five of the islands' six lighthouses, on Raspberry, Sand, Devils, Outer, and Michigan Island, are given by park staff.
- Commercial fish camp tours are given on Manitou Island.
- Campfire programs and nature walks are given on Stockton Island.
- Popular ways to explore the Apostles are by sailboat and kayak.
- The Sea Caves are among the most popular sights.
- You can camp (with a permit and fee) on 18 of the islands.

Along the Lake Superior coast of the Apostle Islands National Lakeshore.

In order to further acquaint you with this marvelous national treasure, here are some answers to some frequently asked questions.

What do most visitors do when they visit the islands? Typically, there are around 170,000 visitors to the islands each year, with about 85 percent of them coming between June and September, although the lakeshore is open year-round. Many visitors sail, canoe, and kayak the waters around the islands. Others hike and bike on designated trails. There are over 50 miles of maintained trails among the islands. Most of these are on Stockton Island (14.5 miles), while Oak Island has 12 miles, Outer has 9 miles, and Basswood 7.5 miles. Manitou, Sand, Rocky, and Otter all feature trails of less than 3 miles. Off-road biking and ATV riding is not allowed anywhere in the islands.

How much time does one need to explore the islands? If you're going to camp, explore the woods and water, and visit some of the islands' historical and cultural sites, allow one to three days. Of course, you can spend a month here and not exhaust the many possibilities for new discoveries. To get a flavor of the islands without roughing it, many visitors often take the ferry to Madeline Island, tour the historical museum, take in lunch, browse through a couple of shops, drive out to one of the parks, then return to the mainland the same day.

Lake Superior coast of the Apostle Islands National Lakeshore.

This swimmer doesn't mind the cool waters of Lake Superior.

What islands have exhibits and cultural centers? There are visitor centers on Little Sand Bay on the mainland, and Stockton Island. On South Twin Island there is the Hokenson Brothers Fishery museum as well as a contact station. Manitou Island has the Manitou Island Fish Camp.

What about bugs and bears? Bugs that bite love these islands, especially

143

between May and August. While walking in the woods, bring plenty of insect repellent and wear long pants that fit snugly at the ankles. Black bears live on several islands. Stockton Island, a popular camping destination, has a large bear population. So, to avoid encounters with them, keep your campsites clean and make sure you don't leave food out as an invitation for bears to partake.

Managed by the National Park Service, excursion boats take visitors back and forth between the islands from June through mid-October. The park's year-round headquarters is located in Bayfield's Old County Courthouse.

The _Island Princess_ cruises the Apostle Islands.

Visitors should make this a must-stop for getting acquainted with the islands and deciding where to go. While there, you can view a film, a variety of exhibits, and other interesting island information. **To learn more about these fascinating islands, contact Apostle Islands National Lakeshore. Route 1, Box 4, Bayfield, 54814. (715) 779-3397**

Getting Around

Apostle Islands Water Taxi. Available to take campers on a round-trip to designated campsites. (715) 779-5153.

Inner Island Shuttle. Go north of Bayfield to Little Sand Bay to the shuttle departure area. Shuttle operates a few days a week between specific islands, most recently, Raspberry, Sand, and Oak. (715) 779-3925.

Apostle Islands Cruise Service. The _Island Princess_, a two-deck excursion boat run by a Coast Guard licensed crew, offers several different cruises around the 22 Apostle Islands from mid-May to mid-October. There's the Sunday Brunch Cruise, Grand Tour, and several others.

**The dramatically eroded Squaw Bay Sea Caves,
north of Bayfield, along the shores of Lake Superior.**

I took the four-hour Lighthouse/Squaw Bay Sea Caves evening cruise. We passed Stockton Island, where there are more black bears, per size of the area, than any other place in the eastern half of the country (and they swim from island to island and back and forth from the mainland). On Raspberry Island, the lighthouse keeper is known to dress up in a uniform from the 1930s when giving tours. About an hour and a-half into the cruise we passed Sand Island, where a gothic lighthouse was built from local stone in 1881. The Squaw Bay Sea Caves, a long string of dramatically sculptured caverns set along the mainland's coast, were the cruise's highlight and alone worth the trip. Offices for the cruises are at Bayfield's City Dock. At the height of the summer season, buy tickets in advance. (715) 779-3925.

Inside Lake Superior's fascinating Squaw Bay Sea Caves in winter.

145

Madeline Island

Twenty minutes via car ferry from Bayfield, Madeline Island is the most accessible—and largest—of the Apostle Islands. Madeline was once the home of the Ojibwa, then a settlement for the European fur traders and missionaries, and since the 1900s a resort community. Today, there are about 150 year-round residents, with that number swelling to about 2,500 in the summer.

It is interesting to note that Madeline, the most frequently visited among the islands, is not included in the national lakeshore designation. There have been year-round residents on Madeline for more than 100 years, and because there still are a number of people who live on the island throughout the year, Madeline cannot be designated as a national park.

Visitors can browse through this building at the Madeline Island Historical Museum.

When traveling in other areas, you've undoubtedly seen ads that insist you visit some attraction and, indeed, make you feel guilty if you haven't. Now, no one is pushing you to visit Madeline Island, but if you don't go, you'll never know what you missed. Visiting the island is a wonderful way to envision what life must have been like in these far northern communities long ago. There are several restaurants here, fewer than a dozen places to stay, and a fine golf course at Madeline Island Golf Club. But most visitors come to visit the Madeline Island Historical Museum and to sail, hike, fish, or explore the beaches, coves, and forests. The island has a rustic beauty and charm not often equaled elsewhere. Take Grampa Tony's, for instance, a friendly restaurant serving pizza, burgers, and salads near the docks in LaPointe, the island's only town. When was the last time you saw a big cardboard box filled with bags of chips and a sign saying "Free"? There was something else that was small-town comfortable about this place. At the rear of the restaurant, a large credenza held new and used books for sale, mostly under $2.

Getting to Madeline Island in the winter is half the fun. When the lake is partially frozen, a windsled, a propeller-driven boat, is used to convey passengers and cargo. Between January and March, when the water is usually frozen solid, the route becomes an "ice road" that can support cars and snowmobiles. This is the main route for schoolchildren and mail going back and forth. Winter visitors can join or behold the "Run on Water," a five-mile run between Bayfield and the island. Hearty folks run, walk, or snowshoe on ice the first Saturday in February. **For more information, call the Madeline Island Chamber of Commerce, (715) 747-2801.**

Sights and Attractions

Madeline Island Ferry Line. Takes you and your car on a scenic twenty-minute trip between Bayfield and the docks at LaPointe. Operates as long as the water is open and navigable, usually April through December. Call for specific times. (715) 747-2051.

Madeline Island Historical Museum. Walk in the footsteps of the early explorers. Near the front entrance, don't miss the 20-minute slide show. It's a haunting and in-

Hypothermia

Lake Superior is a very clean, cold lake. In the summer, the average lake temperature offshore of Bayfield hovers around 54 degrees. However, during some summers the water is significantly warmer and swimming is possible in July and August. Bayfield has two beaches—one between Cooperage and Ferry Landing and the other next to Boutin's Fisheries at the end of Washington Avenue.

In this and other northern lakes, it's important to know what to do to avoid hypothermia, a life-threatening condition that prevents the body from functioning normally. When hypothermia sets in, the body's temperature sinks to dangerously low levels. Follow these simple rules when you're boating or swimming in cold-water lakes:

• If the air is warm, don't assume the water temperature is the same.
• The water temperature should be around 82 degrees for swimming, the air temperature about 3 degrees higher.
• If you start shivering or have blue lips, get out of the water immediately.
• If you suspect someone has hypothermia, remove his or her wet clothes, wrap the person in blankets and dry clothes, and give him or her hot liquids. Don't offer alcohol or coffee. Keep watch over the person, and if there isn't improvement within a short time, contact the closest medical center.

The Madeline Island Historical Museum has many interesting exhibits showcasing local history and artifacts.

triguing narrative, educational, and fun to watch as images move between three different screens. Many visitors comment that the small but terrific museum is one of Wisconsin's best. Open daily, Memorial Day through the first week of October. A short walk up the hill from the ferry dock at La-Pointe. (715) 747-2415.

Big Bay State Park. This beautiful state park was established in 1963 and encompasses 2,350 acres. The park, on the opposite side of the island seven miles from the LaPointe ferry dock, offers excellent opportunities for beach exploration along Barrier Beach and nearby Big Bay Lagoon. The park is also a favorite area with campers. Hike, bike, camp, fish, or picnic—Big Bay is an outstanding scenic area for all these activities. Bayfield telephone: (715) 779-4020; island telephone: (715) 747-6425.

Big Bay Town Park. This other wild and wonderful park is directly opposite Big Bay State Park. The glorious beaches are dotted with boulders—just part of the inspiring landscape. Hiking, biking, camping, and exploring opportunities abound here.

Washburn

Washburn, sometimes described as the "Little City on the Big Lake," is located on Chequamegon Bay. This historic community, the county seat of Bayfield County, knows how to exude small-town charm. Situated between Bayfield 12 miles to the north and Ashland to the south, the community has a rich history. Native Americans from eight nations once lived in the area before the explorers, fur traders, trappers, and missionaries established roots. Between 1880 and the 1920s, Washburn was a boom town because of its strong link with the logging industry. After the Great Chicago Fire, Washburn played an important role in helping rebuild the Windy City.

At Washburn's heart is the Washburn Historical Museum and Cultural Center, which preserves the stories and character of Washburn's shoreline history. Area recreation includes the Mt. Valhalla recreation area northwest of town on County C. Hike or ride horseback in the summer, and in the winter come in from the cold and spread out in front of the fire pit. Snowshoe, cross-country ski, or ride snowmobiles on the area trails. Fish from Washburn's piers before the ice freezes, then join ice-fishing aficionados in the bay. Fishing for coho and chinook is superb in the protected waters of Chequamegon Bay. **For more information call the Washburn Chamber of Commerce, (715) 373-5017 or (800) 253-4495.**

Big Bay State Park on Madeline Island.

Sights and Attractions

State Fish Hatchery. Here's where you get your chance to see what's swimming in the big, deep blue beyond. Several types of fish are produced here, including salmon and lake trout. North of town on WI 13 between Washburn and Bayfield. Open April through December. (715) 779-4021.

Washburn Historical Museum and Cultural Center. This magnificent brownstone structure, also known as the Old Bank Building, was built in 1890 and is now listed on the State and National Register of Historic Places. History unfolds as exhibits trace early settlers' family trees and explain the area's former industries, such as the interesting DuPont Dynamite Plant. Art

149

shows and concerts are featured in the Cultural Center. Exceptional gift shop. 1 E. Bayfield Street. Free taxi service in summer. Open every day during summer. Between October and May, hours vary. (715) 373-5591.

U.S. Forest Service. If you want to book a campsite in the nearby Chequamegon National Forest, check with the Forest Service headquarters in Washburn. The staff is also a good resource for directing you to area boating, hiking, fishing, cross-country skiing, and snowmobiling. P. O. Box 578, Washburn, 54891. (715) 373-2667.

Out to Eat

It's A Small World Restaurant. You might not know it by driving by, but this is one of the most imaginative road stops around. As restaurants go, this is a mini-United Nations. Each week, an assortment of ethnic dishes is featured from a rotating list of national favorites. Still haven't found what you want? There's always the Oddball Burger, supposedly named for Mr. Oddball, a former proprietor. 144 W. Bayfield. (715) 373-5177.

Shopping

Chequamegon Book and Coffee Co. Features a huge number of new, used, and discounted books, around 50,000 according to the last count; they are easy to browse through since they're organized by subject and alphabetized by author. Good expresso and cappuccino. Across from the historical museum. 2 E. Bayfield Street. (715) 373-2899.

Ashland

About 30 minutes south of the Apostle Islands and 60 miles east of Superior lies Ashland, the largest town in this part of the state. In the mid-1600s the Ojibwa were living in the area along with French missionaries. Not surprisingly, Ashland became a transportation boom town due to its prime location along six miles of Lake Superior shoreline. With the growth of the mining and shipping industries, by the late 1890s Ashland had earned a reputation as being a primary ore-shipping center. With the exception of Duluth and Superior, the port was shipping more ore than any other city in the Midwest.

Today, Ashland is known as a wonderful place to relax and rejuvenate. The community of approximately 8,700 residents is often called "Lake Superior's Hometown." Drive through Ashland and you'll see many fine old homes and buildings constructed of native brownstone (they stand out because of the stone's resemblance to Southwestern red clay). Ashland was once home to several brownstone quarrying companies, so it's no coincidence that so many structures are made of that material; the Ashland City Hall, listed on the Register of Historic Places, is one fine example. The producers of the movie *A Simple Plan*, with Bridget Fonda and Billy Bob

Thornton, liked the look of the town too. They shot part of the movie on location here in the winter of 1997.

The east side of Ashland offers splendid panoramic views of the Apostle Islands and the city's old lighthouse on the breakwater. For an interesting walk, go out on the causeway and take in the harbor and the mammoth Soo Line Ore Dock on Water Street. This remnant of Ashland's heyday as a mining and shipping center is the largest dock of its kind in the world.

Then take time to scout out the historic district downtown. Two blocks from the waterfront, many historically significant buildings have found new life as gift shops, restaurants, and retail shops.

One of the most interesting things going on in Ashland today is its "timeless timber" industry. Over 100 years ago many log rafts sank in Chequamegon Bay on their way to market. Today, these virgin logs are being retrieved from the lake's bottom and are finding new markets with artists and craftspeople who use this exceptional old timber in their work.

If you're staying in Ashland and want to experience more of Wisconsin's scenic outdoors, you're only 30 minutes from from beautiful Copper Falls State Park (see chapter 4). **Ashland Area Chamber of Commerce, 320 4th Avenue West. Located in the Bay Area Civic Center. (800) 284-9484.**

Sights and Attractions

Ashland Historical Society Museum. The magnificent 15-room Wilmarth mansion, built in 1869, now houses this fine museum. Absorb the mansion's Victorian charm and Ashland's first 100 years from the displays and exhibits. It's a good place to lose yourself in Ashland's past. Open Monday through Saturday. 522 Chapple Avenue. (715) 682-7185.

Prentice Park. Ashland is a city of many fine parks. Prentice Park, west of town, is one of the most impressive. Here, an old forest of more than 100 acres has something for everyone. Watch the deer in the deer park, camp at one of the campsites, or walk the boardwalk along Fish Creek Slough.

Sigurd Olson Environmental Institute. Northland College, located in Ashland, is known for its environmental studies program. Visit the Sigurd Olson Institute to take in the fascinating passive solar displays. Usually open Monday through Friday, 8 A.M. to 4:30 P.M. Northland College, 1411 Ellis Avenue (WI 13). (715) 682-1223.

South Shore Brewery. This microbrewery produces fine English ales. Enjoy a tour, then sample a selection over lunch or dinner in the brewery pub. Open daily. In the Depot (formerly the Soo Line Railroad Depot, now converted to shops and restaurants). 400 Third Avenue West. (715) 682-4200.

Event

Whistle Stop Festival. This three-day weekend in mid-October, new in 1998, features music with a different mix. One day is devoted to polka and other ethnic music (Oompahfest), another to blues and microbrews (Saturday Blues and Brews), and on Sunday, the music changes to gospel (Gospel-fest). In addition to the music, there are a variety of other events, including a marathon and a half-marathon, a pig roast, fish boil, and pancakes hot off the grill. Tickets can be purchased for each event or as a three-day pass. Downtown Ashland on Third Street, at the Civic Center. (800) 284-9484.

Lodging

Hotel Chequamegon. Looking more like a European manor house than a hotel, this property was originally built in the late 1800s, then rebuilt in 1986. Regardless of its age, it still looks and feels like a glorious old estate. Great lakeside views, two restaurants (the Molly Cooper and Sirtoli's Steak House), indoor pool, and whirlpool round out an atmosphere embellished with refinements. 101 Lake Shore Drive West. (715) 682-9095 or (800) 946-5555.

The Residenz. A beautiful Victorian bed and breakfast with turreted peaks and commanding front porch. This historical treasure was built in 1889 by Senator C. Lamoreau. A restful setting, with exceptional antiques and a full breakfast. 723 Chapple Avenue. (715) 682-2425.

Shopping

The Antique Inn. If you're looking for antiques and collectibles, this is your sort of place. Since 1972 a treasure trove of rare and unique items has passed through here. Shop for toys, glassware, furniture, even a Tiffany lamp now and then. 2016 E. Lakeshore Drive. (715) 682-5452.

The Cheese House. When in Ashland, stop here for Wisconsin-made products—many are locally produced. House specialties include Wisconsin cheese and sausage, butter fudge, locally grown wild rice, and venison. Adjacent to The Antique Inn. 2014 E. Lakeshore Drive. (715) 682-5452.

index

Best Canoe Trails of Southern Wisconsin
by Michael E. Duncanson

Best Wisconsin Bike Trips
by Phil Van Valkenberg

Great Weekend Adventures
from the Editors of *Wisconsin Trails*

Great Wisconsin Taverns
by Dennis Boyer

Great Wisconsin Restaurants
by Dennis Getto

The W-Files
True Reports of Wisconsin's Unexplained Phenomena, by Jay Rath

The M-Files
True Reports of Minnesota's Unexplained Phenomena, by Jay Rath

The I-Files
True Reports of Illinois' Unexplained Phenomena, by Jay Rath

County Parks of Wisconsin
600 Parks You Can Visit Featuring 25 Favorites, by Jeannette and Chet Bell

Great Wisconsin Walks
45 Strolls, Rambles, Hikes & Treks, by Wm. Chad McGrath

Great Minnesota Walks
by Wm. Chad McGrath

The Wisconsin Traveler's Companion
A Guide to Country Sights, by Jerry Apps and Julie Sutter-Blair

W Is For Wisconsin
by Dori Hillestad Butler and Eileen Dawson

Walking Tours of Wisconsin's Historic Towns
by Lucy Rhodes, Elizabeth McBride, and Anita Matcha

Wisconsin: The Story of the Badger State
by Norman K. Risjord

Paddling Northern Wisconsin
by Mike Svob

Barns of Wisconsin
by Jerry Apps

Portrait of the Past
A Photographic Journey Through Wisconsin 1865-1920
by Howard Mead, Jill Dean, and Susan Smith

Perennial Gardening in the Upper Midwest
by Joan Severa

The Spirit of Door County
A Photographic Essay, by Darryl R. Beers

Foods That Made Wisconsin Famous
by Richard J. Baumann

Wisconsin Tales and Trails, Inc.
P.O. Box 5650 * Madison, WI 53705
(800) 236-8088 * info@wistrails.com